Milwaukee Mayhem

MILWAUKEE MAYHEM

Murder and Mystery in the Cream City's First Century

—◆—

MATTHEW J. PRIGGE

WISCONSIN HISTORICAL SOCIETY PRESS

Published by the Wisconsin Historical Society Press
Publishers since 1855

© 2015 by the State Historical Society of Wisconsin

For permission to reuse material from *Milwaukee Mayhem*
(ISBN 978-0-87020-716-7; e-book ISBN 978-0-87020-717-4),
please access www.copyright.com or contact the Copyright Clearance Center,
Inc. (CCC), 222 Rosewood Drive, Danvers, MA 01923, 978-750-8400.
CCC is a not-for-profit organization that provides licenses and
registration for a variety of users.

wisconsinhistory.org

Photographs identified with WHi or WHS are from the Society's collections;
address requests to reproduce these photos to the Visual Materials Archivist
at the Wisconsin Historical Society, 816 State Street, Madison, WI 53706.

Printed in the United States of America
Designed by Sara DeHaan

17   16   15   14   13   1   2   3   4   5

Library of Congress Cataloging-in-Publication Data

Prigge, Matthew J.
  Milwaukee mayhem : murder and mystery in Milwaukee's first century /
Matthew J. Prigge.
      pages cm
  Includes bibliographical references and index.
  ISBN 978-0-87020-716-7 (hardcover : alk. paper)—ISBN 978-0-87020-717-4
(ebook : alk. paper) 1. Murder—Wisconsin—Milwaukee. I. Title.
  HV6534.M65P75 2015
  364.152'3097759509034—dc23
                                2015007718

Front cover: WHi 49492, the Milwaukee River at night

∞ The paper used in this publication meets the minimum requirements of
the American National Standard for Information Sciences—Permanence of
Paper for Printed Library Materials, ANSI Z39.48–1992.

"Whoever shall record the annals of the circle of States which environ the mighty Lakes of the New World, must occasionally pause from the swelling narrative of a wilderness subdued, of savage and foreign enemies conquered, of Territories and States organized, of the sudden apparition of cities, roads and cultivated fields teeming with population and wealth—from such and similar signs of an unprecedented material development—and pause upon some startling outbreak of human passion, which, though a mere eddy in the mighty current—though only an episode of domestic life—will often be found no less suggestive of instruction than thrilling with interest."

—from *Report of the Trial of Mary Ann Wheeler, for the Murder of John M. W. Lace, Her Seducer*

Contents

◈ VICE ◈

◈ SECRETS ◈

The Orphans of History

I N THE summer of 1845, the young village of Milwaukee spent several weeks tearing itself apart at its riverway seams. While the village had been incorporated more than five years earlier—joining settlements that had grown along each side of the Milwaukee River—the unification was hardly one of spirit or purpose. The most contentious of their disagreements was over the bridges that spanned the waterway. Of the three bridges that crossed the Milwaukee River, those who lived on the west side favored only the one that led down Spring Street, which allowed them access to City Hall and the courthouse. Each of the others were, in their estimation, impediments to river traffic. Those living on the east side preferred the connections that allowed for materials to be unloaded at their lakeside docks and transported across the river by wagon or cart. Westsiders preferred these goods to be unloaded at their river docks, bypassing the east altogether. When a befuddled schooner captain plowed his vessel into the crossing at Spring Street, westsiders accused the east side of paying the captain to cripple their choice passage, revenge for their refusal to help finance the bridges they considered deleterious to their community. Within days, Milwaukee's two halves were at war.

It had been more than two hundred years since Father Jacques Marquette became the first European to see the land the village now occupied. He noted in his diary that the place was of "no value." Dozens of Europeans visited and traded at the spot over the following decades. The first resident of the area was a Frenchman named La Framboise, whose misdeeds with the locals caused him to be chased out of the area in

1791. The first permanent white resident was Jean Baptiste Mirandeau, who arrived in 1795. His reasons for coming are not known, although some whispered that a scandalous love affair sent him to the young nation's hinterlands, while others swore he had taken up the stance of a heretic during his training for the priesthood and fled on the eve of his taking orders. Mirandeau lived east of the Milwaukee River with his Native American wife and large family for nearly a quarter century, trading with local tribes, farming, and operating as a part-time blacksmith. He also might have been Milwaukee's first resident inebriate, as he met his fate in the winter of 1819 when he tried to move a heavy log while drunk.

Around the same time Mirandeau was shuffling through the snow toward his dreary end, a six-foot tall, twenty-five-year-old Frenchman named Solomon Juneau was taking over the fur-trading business of Jacques Vieau, who had been swapping with local tribes in the Menomonee Valley since 1795. But it was more than Vieau's pelt trade in which Juneau was interested. He had also become smitten with his fourteen-year-old daughter, Josette. Solomon and Josette were married the next year and in 1822 built a cabin on the east-side stomping grounds of the ill-fated Mirandeau. For more than a decade, Juneau was contented with the simple life of a frontier trader. His primary efforts toward the growth of the settlement were via his dear wife, Josette, who gave birth to seventeen of his children. No one in the area at the time, least of all Juneau, recorded any visions of the place rising to became a major American city. Then the Yankees began to arrive.

Byron Kilbourn was, in the words of historian H. Russell Austin, "the most accomplished and learned man to appear in the little backwoods community" when he arrived to survey the land west of the Milwaukee River in 1834. He had aristocratic roots and came from an eastern family of means. Kilbourn never intended his career as a surveyor to satisfy his ambitious nature. It was in the course of performing his governmental duties across the river from Juneau's peaceful little outpost that he determined to make himself a city builder. The land west of the waterway, he felt, would prove superior to the swampy patch of earth that Juneau occupied. The Juneau settlement, while having direct access to the lake, was also pinched on three sides between the lake and river. These waterways were almost a noose and, with just the right angling, Kilbourn seemed confident it could be slipped around the neck of the little village, allowing it to hang as his west side birthed a new American metropolis. But Juneau was not one to back down from a fight. For a decade, the earthy, overgrown Frenchman and the refined eastern sharpy built rival villages and competed for the flood of speculation money flowing into the new American west. Juneau called his village "Milwaukie"; Kilbourn called his "Milwaukee." No one knew what the word meant.

Milwaukee's population at the time of Kilbourn's arrival (excluding Native Americans) totaled about twenty. By the time his ward's loyalists took axes to the bridge at Chestnut Street ten years later to avenge the felling of the Spring Street Bridge, nearly nine thousand called the place home. Milwaukee's population had tripled in the preceding three years as teams of men swarmed to the place. These were men familiar with hard ways and bone-breaking work. They had set to the west for no more of a reason than to bleed their fortunes from the fertile frontier. As the east ward awoke the morning after Kilbourn's west ward made its move on Chestnut Street, they found the bridge reduced to a watery pile of mangled timbers. A mob hustled an old cannon that was being used as a decoration piece to the bank of the river and set its aim upon the home of Byron Kilbourn. Lacking cannonballs, they dismantled a nearby clock, and its round weights were loaded into the muzzle.

These were men who had been strangers to this area a few years prior. But their fervid loyalty to their adopted wards suggests a kind of madness was growing amongst those grizzly settlers who had made this swampy patch of earth their adopted home. The dangers of an existence trapped between what was at the time considered civilization and savagery, the desperations of a life teetering between wealth and destitution, and the maddening onward march of progress all seemed to be acting as an invitation to mayhem.

But the cannon remained unfired. Word spread in the east that Byron Kilbourn's young daughter had just died. Not willing to fire upon a home in mourning, the eastsiders instead finished off the Spring Street Bridge, sending the broken link to the west tumbling into the river. Now completely severed of connections to the Kilbourn ward, the Juneau loyalists moved next on the bridge that spanned the Menomonee River, the marshy waterway forming the southern border of the western ward. After leveling this bridge, the easterners marched proudly home, crossing the village's only passable bridge, the crossing at Water Street that linked Juneautown with the lands south of the Menomonee. The west warders might have moved on that bridge as retaliation but were, at the moment, unable to get to it.

The "Bridge War," as the affair came to be known, was settled by the village trustees, the details mashed out in the first city charter, signed in 1846, officially birthing the City of Milwaukee. The city fathers might have guided the quill of peace, but the war that made Milwaukee was fought in the streets by a nameless rabble of men with little to lose, but with everything on the line. It was in these lost souls that the mayhem of the times manifested itself. The Bridge War was but one example of the mayhem bred by the transition of a space to place to city to metropolis.

This is the story of the Milwaukee that finds its home in such mayhem, a story that memorializes the dark places both within itself and within its citizens. A city cannot be built on progress and triumph alone. The march forward leaves a mass of the long-forgotten in its wake. The exceptional few are driven to maddened acts of violence, directed at enemies, lovers, and themselves. Scores more lived honestly and quietly but indulged such wicked acts by following them in the gory details of the daily newspapers. Almost all such acts were roundly condemned, pitied, and mourned. But still they read. Other acts of carnage seemed to be the doings of the city itself, vengeful swipes back at a populace bound and determined to beat the place out of its natural shape and into whatever form fit its ever-changing needs. The sites of these disasters, often still fresh with the blood of the unfortunates, also drew hoards of the morbidly curious. The silent masses who gaped alongside these tragedies spoke for the city that could not stop moving, but also one that was never as far away from its adolescence as it liked to think.

And if there was a thrill in watching, there was also a thrill in hiding oneself. As Milwaukee grew, so did its dark corners. The city took to catering to the darker desires of its people as pocket neighborhoods that specialized in sin grew like saplings, their roots secreting themselves through the place until they were as vital to the city as the grain exchange or the waterworks. Some people were made by these trades, others ruined. But no one could escape the creep of these shadows completely. Not those who indulged in such places, not those who crusaded against them, not even those who hustled past the dark corners and pretended to be unaware of the city's most open dirty secrets.

These stories, and their actors, are the orphans of history. They are too obscure to fit into the standard historical narratives, yet too damn weird to completely ignore. There are few heroes here and even fewer lessons learned. This is an incomplete history, dredged from the memory and prejudices of the times and unable to access those secrets the city still wishes to keep. This is a history that rides that dark and often senseless arc that slices through the daily happenings of a long-forgotten class of killers, liars, and crooks. This is the history of a city's one-hundred-year struggle to leave its past behind, to understand itself, and to make sense of the everyday mayhem of life in a metropolis being born.

MURDER

As the muddy trading pit of Milwaukee tottered to its feet as a major American metropolis, its residents—both those bred here and those just passing through—were occasionally driven to acts of violence as heartbreaking and horrifying as they were mesmerizing. These are stories of blood spilt: one's own or that of another, the warm blood of love or the chilled gore of retribution, blood let in fits of rage and blood whose sticky sheen seemed the only path to peace.

What drove these people to the darkest corners of their own capability is what drives people there still. The commonplace occurrences of sorrow, rejection, fear, and lust—distorted through lenses of shame, hatred, and madness—are what consume many of this chapter's actors.

These doomed actors lived here, died here, and killed here. The commonplace madness that displaced them from the gentle confines of reason still exists in this place. We breathe the air of their final breaths, sleep in the homes they shattered, and travel the roads they stalked. Their Milwaukee has become ours, its earth still in possession of the blood of these unfortunates.

They are our neighbors still.

SLIPPERS AT THE CISTERN
November 1874

MARIA WAGNER was dying. She had taken ill shortly after being abandoned by her husband, left to fend for herself and her young son, Carl. An emergency hysterectomy was needed to save her life, after which she was taken in by her sister and brother-in-law, Mary and Edward Aschermann. Edward was the proprietor of a downtown cigar factory and had once been a business partner of Maria's estranged husband. The couple nursed her during her recovery and provided support for young Carl, allowing them both to stay at their large home at 203 Thirteenth Street. Maria was preparing to remarry when a routine visit to her doctor revealed that her illness had returned. Her death would be a painful one. It could come in as little as two weeks.

In the week after her diagnosis, Maria wrote three letters: one to her mother, one to Edward, and one to the man she had planned to marry. Each letter was an explanation and an apology. To her thirteen-year-old son Carl, "all she had in the world," she wrote nothing. The boy had recently returned from a grand European vacation paid for by his uncle Edward. He toured a boarding school in Germany that he was to attend with a son of the Aschermanns. Maria had evidently signed off on her son's future plans, but now, facing the last days of her life, she was unable to leave him behind.

The Sunday after her diagnosis, Maria was the last in the house to bed. Sometime past midnight, her sister heard her descending the stairs. Into the darkness, she asked who was there. "It is I," Maria replied. She said she was going out to the yard but would return shortly. Mary listened as her sister walked through the house and into the inky blackness of the fall evening. Mary knew about the return of Maria's illness. Although her sister had seemed composed and tranquil over the past days, Mary was worried about her mental state. As five, ten, then twenty minutes passed with no rustling downstairs, Mary grew worried. Finally, she roused Edward and asked him to go out and check on Maria.

Edward lit a lantern and went into the yard. He scanned the grounds but could find nothing. Finally, in the stoic chill of the November air, the glow of his lamp caught something out of place. He slowly approached the mouth of the brick cistern that was buried in the rear of the lot. The lid had been removed from the circular opening that led to its underground belly, which was filled about four feet deep. In the grass just beside the mouth sat a pair of women's night slippers.

A brick cistern similar to the one in which Maria Wagner ended her life
Library of Congress HABS FLA, 17-PENSA, 65-3

As Edward approached the cistern, Mary got up to check on her young daughter, who shared a bedroom with Carl. She found the girl frantically shaking her cousin, trying to wake him. Mary turned her own lantern to the boy's bed and found him foaming at the mouth, his bedclothes covered in blood. Back in the yard, Edward shone a light into the cistern and found Maria floating in a frigid pink pool. Determined that she could not leave her boy, Maria had poisoned the child, secreting him the contents of the empty opiate bottle later found in her bedroom. After putting Carl to bed, she tried feebly to slit her wrists. She drew blood but could not bring herself to cut deeply enough. Blood dripping from her hands, she checked on her boy one last time, went to the yard, and found the cistern.

"BLISS NOT LONG"

September 1897

G EORGE BUNDAY'S parents did not approve of the attention their young son was paying to Blanche Warren. George and Blanche first met as children in Bay City, Michigan. The Bundays were a family of vast means, socially established and protective of their boy. Blanche Warren's family had once been similarly endowed. Her father had been the president of the First National Bank of Bay City, but when the bank collapsed, so did their wealth and standing. The Bundays discouraged George from spending time with the girl, but he had already fallen in the dumb kind of love into which kids often fall.

Eventually, the Bundays moved from Bay City. But George and Blanche kept in touch with an endless series of letters. Her family's limited means forced young Blanche into the working world. She trained as a nurse as George went off to law school at the University of Michigan. After they graduated, fate conspired to reunite the couple. Each accepted a job offer in Chicago and, for the first time in years, George and Blanche could enjoy each other's company. In Chicago, George lived with his parents, who had also relocated to the city. He managed to keep his romance with Blanche secret for a time, but eventually his parents found out, and they encouraged him to end the affair and find a girl more suited to his station. He assured his

mother and father that he would. Days later, a nondescript telegram arrived at the Bunday home. "Am called to Milwaukee on
business. Will return tomorrow. George."

His business in Milwaukee was marriage. The couple arrived
on a Monday afternoon, took a room at the luxurious downtown
Plankinton House hotel, and set out to find a preacher. Milwaukee had long been a destination for Chicagoans in a rush to
the altar. Unlike in Illinois, Wisconsin had no marriage license
requirement. A Milwaukee wedding took no more effort than to
find a willing clergyman. George and Blanche were in such a
hurry and were married that day by Reverend E. A. Brown of
the Christ Episcopal Church at Eighteenth and Wright Streets.
That night, the newlyweds took a few grams of morphine and
enjoyed their first evening in their marital bed.

For the next two days, the couple enjoyed the sights of the
city, the parks and theaters, appearing to the hotel staff as
happy and contented. During this time, George was in touch
with his family in Chicago. The tone and content of their ex-
changes, however, is disputed. His parents later claimed that
he had asked them to see him in Milwaukee but would not say
why. Fearing he might be ill, they pried and he finally confessed
to marrying Blanche. They said that upon learning of the marriage, they asked him to return home and not to bring his new
bride until they had a chance to talk. Blanche later told of a
much more terse exchange. She said they objected vigorously
and told their son she was not welcome in their home. She said
they told him to take a long vacation and forget about his bride.

What was not disputed was that by late Wednesday, George
felt he could not return home with Blanche. The beaming future he had seen as recently as Monday evening—his own practice, homestead, and loving wife—now seemed perilously out of
reach. On Wednesday, after taking in a show at Second Street's
Bijou Theatre, he found a lawyer who kept late hours. He asked
the man to prepare paperwork to transfer all of his real es-
tate holdings to his father. The young man trembled so badly
in the lawyer's office, he had difficulty signing the documents.

"[He was] the most nervous person I ever saw," the lawyer later recalled.

That evening, the couple wrote letters home explaining their decision. As George found a mailbox, Blanche, familiar with the process from her medical training, prepared two syringes with a toxic morphine cocktail. Sometime before midnight, the young lovers took their dose and drifted off to sleep. Blanche eventually woke up. George never did.

The next morning, weak and disoriented, Blanche managed to ring for a bellboy. A doctor was summoned, but she was barely able to explain what had happened. George was already dead. By the next day, the Chicago papers were reporting sensational claims about the suicide of young Bunday. The stories depicted the young man's parents as unwilling to accept his bride, owing to her profession and social rank. After hurrying to Milwaukee, the Bundays sought out a *Milwaukee Journal* reporter to correct these claims. "Oh, it is an awful thing," George's mother told the reporter. "He was such a noble boy. So good and true and noble and honest. If it had been some young girl we would have blamed him and not her." She went on to say that it was her age, not her class, that most upset the family. George was twenty-five years old. No explicit mention of Blanche's age was ever printed, but a letter to the editor in the *Chicago Tribune* from Blanche's brother claimed she was just two years older than her departed groom.

The Bundays collected their son's body and returned to Chicago with his widow still recovering in their honeymoon suite. She was strong enough to travel after a few days but found herself without the funds to pay the hotel bill. She finally managed to wire friends for the cash and set off to return home. As Blanche gathered the sad mementos of her tragic honeymoon, the family of George Bunday laid the young man to rest. No one bothered to tell Blanche about the service. She was still not welcome in the Bunday home.

"OUR COFFINS WILL ARRIVE
AT YOUR HOUSE TODAY..."
January 1905

I N THE summer of 1904, a man took a room at the Groves
Boarding House in Chicago. He presented himself as Mr. E.
S. Terry, a wealthy and refined Englishman. He was, in real-
ity, Arthur Milligan, an English-born Brooklynite, wanted by
police for passing bad checks in Manhattan and for thieving the
payroll at the *Boston Journal* while working there as a clerk. E.
S. Terry was but one of the half-dozen or more aliases possessed
by this man who had empty pockets, spellbinding charm, and
suicidal tendencies.

In Chicago, Milligan took an interest in Florence Groves,
the nineteen-year-old daughter of his landlords. Groves worked
during the day as a telephone switchboard operator, but her
evenings quickly became occupied by the man she knew as
Mr. Terry. She enjoyed singing as he played the house's parlor
piano. Her friends said she was "mesmerized" by him and had
fallen into a kind of awestruck love. Despite her boundless affections, Milligan's insecurities ate at him. He was convinced
that he had a rival for her affections. At least once, he threatened to kill himself if she ever left him.

On Friday, January 13, 1905, after several months of courtship, Milligan and Groves rode the passenger steamer *Indiana*
north to Milwaukee. Groves was under the impression the trip
was a pleasure excursion, but Milligan had far different plans.
They would be wed in Milwaukee, he told Groves during the
trip north. In Milwaukee, the couple took a room at the downtown Blatz Hotel at Water and Oneida[1] Streets, registering as
Mr. S. F. Berry and wife. But sometime during their first nights

---

1. Now Wells Street

in the city, Milligan had a fateful change of heart. The idea of possessing his dear Florence via the bounds of matrimony was no longer enough. The only way to truly make her his own would be to cross with her into the great hereafter. Groves accepted this plan, according to Milligan, willingly—even eagerly—and they made plans to end their lives after nightfall. But when nightfall came, they lost their nerve. The next day, they made the same vow but, again, could not bring themselves to comply. Finally, they agreed to pool their cash and live in high spirits until poverty forced their hand.

After ten days in the city, their money finally ran out. Milligan said that on that day, a Sunday, Groves made three attempts to poison herself. He said that she "begged" him to allow her to go first, saying that she could not bear to live, even for just a few minutes, in a world without him. She swallowed glasses of iodine and wood alcohol but could not keep either down. Early the next morning, Milligan made fifty cents begging and went to a local druggist where he talked the clerk into selling him a bottle of carbolic acid. After mailing a letter to the Groves family, he went up to their room at the Blatz and prepared Florence's dose. He served it to her in a wine glass, helping her in her weakened state to raise it to her mouth.

The young woman's death was a horrifying one. She twisted in pain and writhed grotesquely as the liquid slowly burned away at her viscera. The girl died just past 6:00 a.m. Milligan later said he was reading the newspaper as Groves passed on but also claimed to have been so distressed by her awful demise that he lost the nerve to end his own life. For the next three hours, Milligan remained in the room, trying to work up the nerve to follow her into the excruciating hereafter. "After I saw Florence die in such great agony in my presence," he said, "I could not bear the thought of being found dead with my eyes and mouth open, looking so ghastly." So he fled. He cleaned Groves up and kissed her good-bye. After checking for mail at the front desk, he took a drink in the hotel bar and caught a train out of town.

That afternoon, his letter arrived in Chicago. "We are too divinely happy to live," it read in Milligan's hand. "When you receive this, we will be on our way to heaven. Our coffins will arrive at your house today.... We will die smiling. Bury us side by side." Groves's brother was enraged. He was certain that Milligan—Terry to him—had murdered his sister. He went at once to Milwaukee and arrived at the Blatz as police were clearing out the room. Two more notes were found, both written by Milligan, requesting the bodies be returned to Chicago. By now, the police had discovered Milligan's true identity and a statewide manhunt was launched for his arrest on the charge of murder.

The next day, after a bartender who recognized his photo from the newspaper called police, Milligan was arrested in a Racine flophouse. As the cops broke through his door, Milligan tried in vain to take his dose of poison, but an officer knocked the bottle from his grasp. Saved from death by his own hand, he settled into an odd calm. At the central station in Milwaukee, he asked for—and was given—a swallow of whiskey before laying out his confession. He had planned to escape back to Boston, he told police. There, he would surrender on the standing embezzlement charges against him—under another alias—and hopefully make Arthur Milligan vanish. That June, he was convicted of manslaughter and given ten years at Waupun State Prison. "It is believed," the *Racine Daily Journal* reported, "that he will commit suicide at the first opportunity offered in the prison."

STRAIGHT RAZOR
June 1851

JAMES JOHNSTON, a tall, auburn-haired man of about thirty years, stood in a dank holding cell of Milwaukee's little stone jailhouse, waiting for his turn with the straight razor. It was Sunday morning, the day that the prisoners were permitted to shave. Johnston and his accomplice, a man named Peter King, had been arrested the week before on a burglary charge. The pair had been working together for several years but had till then avoided the censure of the law. Johnston had been known to proclaim that he would sooner take his own life than serve a jail sentence. As the razor was passed from man to man, Johnston waited patiently. Passed the blade, he opened it and proceeded to gently shave his face. His wife, whom he had written of his arrest, was on her way to him and was to arrive later that day. Finishing the job, he kept the blade open, extended his arm, and drove it violently across his throat. The force of the blow tore open his windpipe and sent blood burping from the wound. His fellow prisoners screamed for the jailer, who quickly arrived and looked upon the scene in horror. Johnston stood erect, throat opened and drenched in blood. The jailer rushed into the cell and tried to close the wound with his hand. Johnston fought him back and, for a moment, the two grappled in the deathly red puddle. While a doctor was summoned, Johnston was restless. He lay down, stood, and paced until weakened, then lay again before getting up to pace some more. Within an hour, he was dead. His wife arrived in time to claim the corpse.

"THE GREAT JUDGE"
June 1899

"TODAY, I learned what kind of woman [my wife] is. She misused me and acted wrongly. I have seen it. What kind of man would take such a punishment if he had a certainty as to the facts? She shall die with me." These were the lines written on a single-page letter, folded and kept in the pocket of Fred Gmelin as he sat in the saloon at 623 West Walnut Street that he owned with his wife. The night before, the Gmelins had one of the many rows that punctuated their brief marriage.

Fred stomped off in anger after the fight but had returned that morning to settle the matter. He found that his wife was out, so he sat and waited.

Fred and Victoria Gmelin were an atypical couple. They met when he hired her as a housekeeper after his first wife died. As he sat in wait with the letter in his pocket, he was sixty-two, she just twenty-eight. Despite the age gap and the regular domestic squabbles, the marriage had produced two sons, two and four years old. The present situation had peaked about three months earlier. Fred, fraught with jealousies over the attention that younger men paid his pretty, young wife, left the home and moved in with an adult son from his first marriage, leaving Victoria to care for the children and run their saloon. In March, she had Fred arrested on charges of spousal abandonment. In turn, he brought a suit of divorce against her.

When Victoria returned home, Fred said nothing. She set up an ironing table and began work on the chores. He sat, watching her work, while his young children played at her feet. Without a word, he rose, drew a .32-caliber revolver from his jacket, and fired two shots into her midsection. As his wife fell into a heap, he turned the pistol into his mouth and fired once. The gun barrel was still clamped between his teeth as he fell dead to the floor. Victoria, wounded and bleeding, gathered herself and ran into the street, her two boys close behind. From two sharp holes in the steel corset cinched about her waist, crimson streams of blood soaked her dress. Outside, she collapsed into the arms of a passerby.

Victoria was rushed to a doctor, who quickly determined she would survive the attack. Had the slugs not been slowed by her heavy corset, she might not have been so fortunate. That afternoon, as the bullets were being plucked from Victoria's ribs and Fred was hauled off to the morgue, their divorce case was to be heard by the judge. The pending case was closed, the *Milwaukee Journal* noted, "when the great judge, Death, granted the divorce."

THE MARRYING BRAKEMAN
May 1931

"**G**ET ALL togged out like I am.... Keep well-shaved and kid the women along. You'll be surprised how quickly they will fall.... Then a little moonlight, sweet words whispered in their ears, and you've got 'em on their way to get a marriage license. A couple of weeks more to find out how much dough they've got and you'll have it. Then you can always leave 'em."

This was the advice of George "Jiggs" Perry, to a pal, on how to win big with women. The quote was relayed to the *Milwaukee Sentinel* in October 1930 as a nationwide dragnet had just been launched for Perry, who had wooed, won, and left as many as ten women across the Midwest over the preceding year. At least four of these women claimed that Perry had married them. Another, Cora Belle Hackett, a twice-widowed Milwaukeean who had married Perry in Canton, Ohio, was found dead on the Lac du Flambeau Indian Reservation with a single bullet in her head. She was last seen trudging into the woods with Perry, who was armed with a borrowed rifle, later returned to its owner with a single empty shell in its chamber.

Jiggs Perry was an unlikely Romeo. Thirty-seven years old when he started his marrying spree, Perry was stout and moonfaced. His hair was so badly thinning that he would dunk his head in well water as often as a dozen times a day and walk outside hatless in an attempt to stimulate its growth. Newspapers made references to his having a glass eye. And he worked, when he worked, as a simple railroad brakeman.

Perry's first—and only legal—marriage was to Miss Mary Nickels, whom he wed in 1912 at age nineteen. Together, they had three children and kept a modest home at 1117 Pierce Street in Milwaukee. Even to Mary, Jiggs was known as a flirt who adored the attention of women. He possessed a charm and engaging nature that belied his unimpressive appearance. He was also well read and was said to be able to "talk on any-thing." With a particular interest in the macabre, he made a habit of saving newspaper clippings of murders and was quick to spout off to friends about the mistakes the killer had made. According to Mary, sometime in the late 1920s he suffered an accident that fractured his skull. "Since that time," she later said, "he has been doing some thoughtless things that others criticized, and I excused."

In 1928, Perry left his wife and family. He first went south, spending time in New Orleans before working his way up to New York City. But by early 1929, Perry had come up with a new means of making a living. For the next year, he traveled through Illinois, Ohio, and Wisconsin, finding well-to-do middle-aged women, winning their affections, and "marrying" them, feigning his way through the required paperwork and ceremo-nial trimmings. He posed as a man of means, often showing the women phony letters to himself from prominent Milwaukee cit-izens, congratulating him on his nonexistent business success-es and making vague plans to get together soon on his equally imaginary yacht. After a quick wedding—Perry claimed later it was always the women, never he, who proposed—Perry would leach money and favors from the women, speaking of large sums soon due to him that would make true everything he had prom-ised during their courtship. He would then laze about until the woman got wise or the cash ran out. Then he was on to the next, and the next, and the next....

Katherine Gebhardt was the first, marrying Perry in Janu-ary 1930 in Chicago and setting up a home with him in Cleve-land. During a trip away from Gebhardt to visit an "aunt," Perry met and married Cora Hackett. The couple took their fateful honeymoon that summer at a country resort near the Lac du Flambeau Indian reservation in Eagle River. It was there that Perry borrowed the rifle and marched into the woods with Hack-ett. Later that day, Perry returned to their cabin alone, packed both his clothes and hers, and quickly left. When he got back to Cleveland, Gebhardt was convinced that he had been seeing another woman during his time in Wisconsin. To help win back her trust, Perry gave her a trunk of fine, new clothes—those that once belonged to the departed Cora Hackett.

The marriage to Gebhardt ended when another woman called her and asked if she was married to Perry. Gebhardt replied that she was, causing the other woman to exclaim, "Why, that can't be! He proposed to me and promised me eighteen thousand dollars after we were married in Chicago!" After parting with Gebhardt, Perry added two more wives to the roster, marrying Lida Downey and Elizabeth Morrison just weeks apart in Camari and Albion, Illinois, respectively. With a deserted wife in Milwaukee, one demanding a divorce in Cleveland, two newlyweds just forty miles apart in Illinois, and the body of Cora Hackett rotting in the Wisconsin North Woods, Perry met and became engaged to Harriet Milligan, a St. Louis widow. They were married shortly before Hackett's body, which had been found a few weeks earlier, was finally identified. When the police made their suspect known, Perry fled to the south, leaving behind three active marriages and at least two pending engagements.

Perry's whereabouts remained unknown until May 1931 when, after reading an article on the case in a true-crime pulp magazine, a San Francisco police officer recognized the grainy image of Perry. In San Francisco, he was known as Frank Moran, husband of thirty-nine-year-old Anna Gutierrez, a former beauty queen and the heiress to a Salvadorian coffee empire. The officer was familiar with Moran, having recently investigated a theft at an apartment building owned by Gutierrez. The couple had been wed in January 1931, which would have been Perry's sixth marriage in twelve months.

After conferring with authorities in Wisconsin, San Francisco police arrested the man known as Moran, who denied knowing anything about anyone named Perry or Hackett. The suspect was held while a Wisconsin detective rushed westward. With the detective was William Parker, the man who owned the resort where Hackett was killed and a personal friend of Jiggs Perry. After arriving in San Francisco, the two men met with the suspect, who continued to insist he was none other than Frank Moran. Parker immediately recognized the man as Perry and recounted numerous stories of their time together. "You're Perry and you know you're Perry," Parker scolded him. "You were with me in 1929 and you were with me in 1930. I and my wife treated you like a brother. We liked you, Perry, and we know you."

But as the suspect refused to relent, a minor slip of the tongue revealed his true identity. At some point during the interview, the suspect referred to Parker as "Bill." The suspect did not catch the gaffe, but the detective did. He stopped the suspect and told him that no one had yet mentioned Mr. Parker's first name. How would Frank Moran know the first name of a man he had never met? The suspect slumped. He admitted nothing but stopped claiming to be Frank Moran. Days later, he was on a train bound east to be charged with the murder of Cora Belle Hackett. The suspect was decidedly dispirited, but perhaps most so because his dear Anna had refused to come see him at the jail. "Take him away. Take him to Wisconsin," Gutierrez told reporters. "I loved him. I think I love him now, but I do not want to see him."

A *Milwaukee Sentinel* reporter rode back with the suspect who, upon being loaded into the train, again began to insist he was Moran and denied ever having suggested otherwise. But the man whose gift of gab had earned him so much love and affection simply could not stop talking and, yet again, his ratchet jaw would run faster than his mind. Urged on by his cabin mates, the suspect talked at length about a number of topics. Somewhere in the Rocky Mountain region, the suspect began to tell a boastful fishing tale that caught Parker's attention. "That happened at my place!" he interrupted.

The suspect sank in his chair. "Oh, what's the use," he sighed. "I'm Perry and you know it.... I'm guilty of bigamy, plenty guilty. But I'm no murderer." On the rest of the long ride back home, Perry was unable to keep quiet about his exploits and romantic conquests. "The women love me. Every woman I ever married loved me. And everything these women gave me they gave of their own free will," he said. He held a particular reverence for Anna and was still stung by her rejection of him. "I suppose that is what they call retribution. The one woman I really loved leaving me alone when I needed her the most." When asked why he embarked on his marrying spree, he was glib but guarded. "Why buy a horse when you can ride for free?" he asked. "I never left any woman until I had to. I never left until I couldn't get any more money from her.... A fine bunch of fools. They could have checked up on me in a hurry."

After arriving in Chicago, he was put into a car and driven north. Just across the Wisconsin border, the car was stopped and Perry was formally charged with murder. Several hours later, he was taken to the Eagle River jail. He was upbeat, certain at least one of his old wives would come to his defense and provide him with the money he now desperately needed. But the only Mrs. Perry to come forward was the first. She made the long trek to Eagle River so his children could see their father. Her statements in support of Perry had been numerous, but she was near broke, frazzled, and paranoid from the attention the case had brought her. She claimed she could not go see her husband upon his arrival in Chicago because her "enemies" there sought to kill her. "Why did you marry all those women, George?" she asked him at the jailhouse. "Why did you do it?"

"Well . . ." was his only reply.

Perry's trial began later that month. He promised an impenetrable alibi but could produce none. He said that he and Hackett had parted in the woods and someone else must have shot her after he left. He claimed to have been overtaken by tears when he heard that Hackett was dead. He said he regretted his spree and wanted badly to return to his first wife (whom he mistakenly referred to as Katherine—his first bigamous spouse). Perry collapsed when he was read the guilty verdict. A few weeks later, he was given a life sentence. Mary Perry maintained that her husband was innocent as he was carted off to the prison at Waupun. No comment was heard from Anna Gutierrez, whom Perry planned to return to after his exoneration. On the train back from California, brimming with confidence about his prospects, he had told a reporter with a grin, "She is waiting for me at the Golden Gate."

LOVE WITH A BULLET
April 1886

ISIDOR SEIDENBAUM was just fifteen when his parents boarded him onto a US-bound ocean liner and said good-bye. In his homeland of Austria, the boy was considered an incorrigible. His family hoped that fending for himself in a new land might straighten out the boy's crooked ways. The plan seemed to work, for by 1886, he was in school in Milwaukee, tutoring children in Hebrew, and was soon to relocate to Cincinnati, where he would complete his degree and finish his rabbinical training. He was still just seventeen years old, with dark hair, deep-set eyes, and a slender build. He was "clean-cut and refined," the newspapers would later say, with the looks of a boy "accustomed to refinement and culture."

But Seidenbaum was also in a troublesome kind of love. He had evidently become infatuated with a student of his, a pretty, young girl, "well-rounded," and "a picture of loveliness." She was Annie Rosenstein, the fourteen-year-old daughter of a local tailor. Seidenbaum had been a frequent visitor to the Rosenstein home, a handsome two-story house at the corner of Vliet and Sixth, in the weeks before his scheduled departure. One night, after playing cards with some members of the Rosenstein family late into the evening, Seidenbaum was invited to stay the night. It is possible he lingered a bit longer than usual that night, hoping to be asked to stay. He carried with him that evening a peddler's pack containing, among other things, a loaded pistol. He gladly accepted the invitation and readied for bed.

Seidenbaum slept with a cousin of the family on the first floor of the house. Annie slept with her four sisters in a room down the hall. At 1:30 a.m., Seidenbaum crept through the house, entered the room, and placed his pistol to the girl's temple. A single shot ended her life. Isidor then turned the gun on himself, placing its barrel to his heart and firing. Awoken by the revolver's report, Annie's parents lit a lamp and quickly found the terrible scene. Their daughter dead, her killer splayed across her bed—blood gushing from his chest and feet dangling to the floor. The look on the dead girl's face was serene. She had passed from life to death without waking. No firm motive was ever established for the crime. An inquest held in the following days could only assume that his love for her had driven him into a state of insanity.

"DON'T DO THAT, HARRY!"
February 1940

MILDRED BELL and Marie Rose walked along Downer Avenue toward the Walgreen's drugstore. Bell and Rose were nursing students, both twenty-two years old and less than a month away from taking their state board exams. They were on a study break, enjoying the mild winter weather, and on their way to get a soda. Beside them, a sedan crept down the street. Behind the wheel was Harry Christiansen, a love-twisted and brooding twenty-two-year-old with a short temper and violent tendencies. Just two weeks earlier, Christiansen had asked Bell to marry him after nearly two years of dating. Bell refused. She told him that she wanted to focus on her career and was not ready to be married. It might have been true, but there were deeper reasons for her rejection.

Christiansen asked the women if they needed a ride. Bell

said they did not and kept walking. The week before, she had tried to break it off completely with Christiansen. He reluctantly agreed to take some time apart from her, but he refused to end the relationship. At least once before, Christiansen had threatened to kill Bell. Her stepfather, Wauwatosa police officer Louis Johnson, had warned the girl that the young man was trouble and urged her to avoid him. Bell had no intention of trying to save the relationship but accepted Christiansen's compromise. The truth was that she was afraid of what he might do if she made him too angry.

Christiansen was the son of Harry Christiansen Sr., president of the General Lumber Company and honorary colonel on the staff of Wisconsin Governor Julius P. Heil. He had briefly attended Purdue University in Lafayette, Indiana, but proved himself a less than stellar academic. During his time in school he was arrested for carrying a .38-caliber revolver. He told police he had purchased the weapon for target shooting, and they returned it to him without filing charges. After failing out of school, he returned home to join the National Guard and work as a salesman for his father. His fascination with weapons had long been known. A friend recalled that he had once used a Thompson sub-machine gun to pepper a car his father had given him. He kept the car and drove it regularly even after the incident. He liked how the bullet holes looked. He was arrested again in 1939 at the Plankinton Arcade in downtown Milwaukee for carrying a handgun and a phony police badge. He begged out of charges once again, telling the officers that it was his dream to join the force and he was studying to take the entrance exam. The cops let him off with a scolding and returned his items. It was the same gun he had carried at Purdue. And it was the same gun he carried as he pulled away from Mildred Bell and Marie Rose as they entered the Downer Avenue Walgreen's.

Inside, the women took a booth and finished off two sodas. At about 1:40 p.m., Bell ordered a malted milk. She was still waiting for her drink when Christiansen pushed through the entrance, half-jogging toward their table. He wore a light sweater and a gun belt. In his clenched hand was his prized .38.

"Don't do that, Harry!" Bell screamed. An instant later he opened fire. Five of his six shots hit Bell. Christiansen executed his assault with chilling efficiency. Bell was struck in the chest, spine, kidney, and head—any of which injuries would have proven fatal on their own—and was dead within seconds. As her head dropped to the table and blood pooled beneath her chair, terrified patrons and staff fled the shop. Rose, briefly frozen with terror, watched as Christiansen emptied the pistol and pulled a single bullet from his belt. "Don't worry," he said. "I won't shoot you." He calmly loaded the bullet into the gun, raised it to his temple, and fired.

As Rose fled, Christiansen fell to the floor in convulsions. The projectile had torn into his brain and lodged behind his right eye. He thrashed about violently on the floor as a waitress called police. Minutes later, the call went out over police radio about a female shot dead by an unknown male on Milwaukee's east side. Bell's stepfather was on patrol when the car radio brought the news. "Boy," he told his partner, "I hope that isn't Mildred." Johnson knew that Mildred frequented the spot and knew her fear of Christiansen. He called the dispatch desk for more details of the shooting and, having confirmed his awful suspicions, went home to tell his wife the terrible news.

Back at the scene, it took several officers to hold Christiansen down as he was handcuffed. He was loaded into an ambulance and rushed to the hospital. Christiansen sat upward during the ride, covered in blood and with the bullet wound in his head still leaking. Asked why he shot Bell, he could only reply, "Leave me alone. I don't know, I don't know. . . ." He finally collapsed at the hospital and lingered near death for the next several days.

Although left sightless by his self-inflicted wound, Christiansen eventually recovered enough to stand trial for his crime. Five months after the shooting, unable to see the judge or jury who decided his fate, he was convicted of murder and sentenced to life in prison.

A.K.A. MARIAN DAVIS
February 1921

"WILL YOU please place these flowers on the coffin of Marian Davis for one who is ashamed to weep beside it?" read the note attached to a bundle of white sweet peas received in the coroner's office. "I want them...to speak to [those] who would let the dying murmur of a broken-hearted girl be: 'It is no use to tell my story—the man has too many friends among officials ever to be punished.'" Lying on the slab that afternoon was the body of a young woman who had finally succumbed to the handful of pills she had swallowed two weeks earlier. "I want them to speak for what I might have been and the joys of life I might have had, but for the vicious things that engulfed me like this girl has claimed." Davis took her fatal dose after an all-night party that made a tour of known spots of sin and vice in the city. Police suspected a quarrel with a lover to be the cause. "I am sir, only, A Painted Girl."

The gaudy circumstances of the suicide and the mysterious nature of its victim made the case a local sensation. No one in Milwaukee seemed to know much about Marian Davis. She was a gentle beauty, "flaxen-haired" and fair. She was rumored to be the daughter of a prominent Green Bay physician, but as she lingered meekly for two weeks at a Milwaukee hospital, no family came to call. Her most regular visitor was Barney Farrell, a well-known roadhouse operator and one of the men alleged to be out with her the evening of her suicide attempt. In the front-page articles the morning after her death, Farrell's lawyer told the press that his client would arrange for the girl's burial.

Marian Davis's real name was Esther Repstine. She was the youngest of ten children, born to a respected and well-off family

in the little farm town of Atchison, Kansas. Repstine was described as "quiet and studious" by friends back home, but the
simple happenings of the prairie were not enough for her. Repstine left home in her late teens—rumors flew that she was with
child—and found work as a telephone operator in Kansas City.
By 1919, she was working in Chicago, still plugging lines by
day and moonlighting as a magazine salesgirl in a hotel. This
was how she met Barney Farrell—the "prince of the Milwaukee nightlife," as he was often called. She moved to Milwaukee
in January 1920, becoming Farrell's "kept woman" and taking
residence at an apartment at 501 Cass Street on which he paid
the rent. To her landlords, she was Mrs. O'Connor, wife to a
considerably older husband who was often out of town and only
spent a few nights each week at home. To everyone else, she became known as Marian Davis.

Farrell spent freely on her, dressing her in furs—including
a two-thousand-dollar mink that draped her shoulders as she
was admitted to the hospital. But if Farrell was easy with his
money, he was tighter with his affections. While Davis was still
living as Esther Repstine, her mother died, leaving the girl so
severely depressed she contemplated suicide. But then she met
Barney. She wrote in a note found after her death that Farrell
"took [my mother's] place," and that he was the only man she
had ever loved. But his love was more elusive. He spent free
hours with his friends and took to drinking every night. Davis
became convinced his associates were trying to get Farrell to
leave her. "I have given up all hope of the future," she wrote,
"but all the world knows I love that man."

The end of her patience with the situation came on January
26, 1921. With Farrell and four others, Davis attended a boxing
match at the city auditorium before touring some of Farrell's
nightspots in an evening of revelry. Witnesses reported that
at some point during the evening, Farrell shoved Davis from
a car and kicked her brutally. After a loud and visible fight at
the LaSalle Hotel at 211 Fourth Street—another spot of ill-
reputation controlled by Farrell—Davis went to a vacant room

while Farrell went to the Cass Street apartment to sleep. Late that night, Davis swallowed seven bichloride of mercury tablets and collapsed. She was found by a pair of Farrell lackeys and dropped at the hospital. "The man in this case," Davis murmured to the police that night, "has so many friends among the officials of this city and the County of Milwaukee that unless I speak, the story will never be known."

But nothing else about the matter would leave her lips. Her condition gradually worsened and detectives, who had been waiting for her to improve, were never able to extract an official statement. Whispers about town suggested she had quarreled with someone named O'Connor, a man who was allegedly posing as her husband to carry on an illicit affair.

Back in Kansas, her family had only vague ideas of the big-city life she was living. She wrote of wearing diamonds about town and sent expensive gifts at Christmastime. But as she lay dying in Milwaukee, it had been several weeks since the family had heard from her. Fearing trouble, Edward Repstine, Esther's older brother, arrived in the city in search of his sister, whom he suspected was living under an assumed name. But Davis had taken efforts to hide her new identity from her family and to portray herself as a young woman without any familial connections. A note found among her things said, "I haven't any people, so don't try to find them." Edward managed to find his sister, but not in time. Davis's body was about to be buried by Farrell when he arrived at the city morgue and identified Marian Davis as his sister.

As police filled the gaps in the sad story of Marian Davis, their interest in Farrell as a suspect was growing. They had already repelled attempts, believed to be made by his associates, to recover the mink coat Davis was wearing when taken to the hospital. Talking to police just days after she was admitted, Farrell said Marian was merely a friend and denied ever being intimate with her. He also denied giving her the bruises that covered her arms and legs—bruises that never healed. In the week after Davis's death, he continued to claim no wrongdoing and denied that he and the mysterious Mr. O'Connor were one and the same. Apparently Farrell did his best to ensure no one else would say otherwise. District attorney Winfred Zabel, exasperated after hearing that a female witness was threatened with death if she spoke against Farrell, exploded in a closed-door interview. "You g[oddamn] dirty bum!" he screamed at Farrell. "What business have you got threatening a woman?"

Finally, after securing testimony from the janitor at the Cass Street apartment who positively identified Farrell as the mysterious Mr. O'Connor, police arrested Farrell at the LaSalle Hotel. The arrest occurred almost exactly one week after Repstine had died and roughly the same moment she was being laid to rest in Kansas. During the next week, more than a dozen raids were executed on various Milwaukee nightspots, a response to the public outcry against conditions that allowed young women like Marian Davis to be led so very far astray. Farrell was later convicted of giving a false statement and given three years in the house of corrections.

LEAVE THE BABY
July 1893

S EAMAN AND Eva Hill were farm kids from the tiny burg of Oak Hill, Wisconsin. They had grown up together, fallen in love, and—just past their twentieth birthdays—stolen away south of the Illinois border to be secretly wed. They chose Milwaukee for their honeymoon destination.

They arrived in the city in time for the Independence Day festivities and enjoyed the plush settings of the newly built Schlitz Hotel and Palm Garden at Grand Avenue and Third Street. But Eva had been keeping a secret from her new husband, one that no woman could keep for long. Sometime after the holiday, she went into labor in their hotel room. Seaman was quite shocked by the development and most certainly watched with bewilderment as the house doctor delivered her baby in the bed of their honeymoon suite. It was not his child.

As stunned as the husband might have been, the trauma of the event and its preceding deceptions sent Eva into an outright panic. She insisted on leaving the hotel immediately, against the forceful objections of the doctor. She wrapped the newborn tightly in a blanket and set off for the lakefront Chicago and North Western depot. The couple lingered along the shoreline for hours. Eva was in fits over the baby. She was horrified at the thought of the shame that would be heaped upon her if she were to return home with a child. Eva told Seaman she needed to rid herself of the baby and said she would throw it in the lake. Seaman objected and tried to stop her, persisting until she said that if he would not allow her to toss away the child, she would jump into the lake herself with the baby firmly in her grip. Somewhere near the flushing station, at the foot of Kane Place, she dropped the newborn into the churning waters. From there, the couple walked back to the depot and boarded a train for Palmyra, Illinois, where they had been married just days earlier.

The Schlitz Hotel, birthplace of the baby Hill
WHi Image ID 54714

The babe's body was found on the beach the next day. Bulletins on the gruesome discovery quickly reached the Schlitz Hotel and officials there alerted police about the Hills. Days later, they were arrested in Palmyra and each casually confessed to the crime. The *Chicago Tribune* reported that neither of them "seemed to realize the enormity of the offense." Each was charged with murder. A postmortem examination of the child, however, revealed that it had already died by the time Eva threw it into the lake. The child had succumbed either to exposure or asphyxiation due to the hotel blanket being so tightly wrapped about its body. Eight months after their arrest, set free on bond and living back home in Oak Hill, the pair pled guilty to a charge of manslaughter. Eva was given one year in the house of corrections. Seaman was fined a hundred dollars.

DEATH BY CANNON
April 1889

J UST BEFORE eight in the morning, fifty-five-year-old Gustav Stenzel sat in the dirt of his backyard assembling a few pieces of cast iron into a makeshift cannon. The device consisted of a small tube, capped at one end with a touch-hole, and packed tightly with gunshot and ball bearings. The night before, Stenzel had arrived home heavily intoxicated. He had threatened his wife, saying he would kill her and then do away with himself. Fraught with terror, Mrs. Stenzel stayed up through the evening. The next morning, Gustav seemed to have regained his sobriety and rationality. Somewhat relaxed, Mrs. Stenzel left the house early in the morning to visit a neighbor. She was still there when Gustav mounted his device on an overturned washtub, knelt in front of it, put his chest to the muzzle, and lit the fuse.

The blast alerted Mrs. Stenzel, who rushed into the yard to find her husband, nearly torn in half by the shot, clinging to his final moments of life with a horrid expression on his face. He muttered something indecipherable before expiring. The cannon, "a novel weapon" in the words of the *Milwaukee Journal*, was found several yards from where he had touched it off.

BINGO
May 1941

ALL THE operator at the Milwaukee telephone exchange could hear were the desperate screams of a violent struggle. The call was traced to room number 608 in a handsome apartment tower at 1104 North Marshall Street. Listening in on what seemed to be a horrible struggle on the other end of the line, the operator phoned the police and told them to send help immediately. Minutes later, officers arrived upon a terrible scene. Fifty-eight-year-old Carrie Seymer, a former music instructor and Sunday school teacher, was dead. Her badly beaten body, dressed in undergarments and a housecoat, lay in a thick puddle of blood, bruises and gashes covering her face. A pair of black gloves had been shoved into her mouth with an "inhuman fury." Bloody splatters and specks covered a wall and continued into a bathroom. A seven-inch section of pipe, the assault weapon, was found on the floor. The receiver had been knocked off the telephone, allowing the operator to audibly witness the awful act. Near the phone, on Miss Seymer's desk, was a receipt for fifty-five dollars' rent paid on one of her many residential properties. No name filled the "received from" blank. It seemed the killer had caught her in the middle of some mundane paperwork.

Initially, the police sought an African American man in the slaying. Several complaints had recently been made in the area about a "heavy-set Negro panhandler." Though nothing had been taken from the apartment, robbery seemed a likely motive. Phone records showed that a call was placed to Seymer from Alice Dornblaser, a tenant of Seymer's who rented an apartment with her husband at 2530 North Fourth Street. Dornblaser said she had contacted her landlord about a receipt for her most recent rent payment. Hers was the name missing from the receipt. Dornblaser said she had also told Seymer of a leaking heating coil. A plumber used by Seymer for maintenance on her properties verified that he had, in the short period between Dornblaser's call and Seymer's murder, gotten a call from Seymer asking him to make the repair.

As police questioned Dornblaser at her home, her thirty-one-year-old daughter Eileen was in the next room. Dornblaser told police she was at home during the time of the killing. Eileen knew it was a lie. She had seen her mother ride off in a taxi shortly after the call to Seymer. She had also recognized the length of pipe found at the scene from a photo in that day's newspaper. She had last seen it on her mother's dresser. Now, it was gone. She said nothing to the police.

While their initial interview turned up no obvious red flags, the police decided to keep an eye on Dornblaser. Her husband and daughter were brought in for separate questioning, and a detective was stationed to observe her little Fourth Street home. Meanwhile, they made a canvass of all city cab companies, checking for any trips to or from the Seymer apartment the day of the murder. Records at the Checker Cab Company found a match. The driver said he had taken a woman from Fourth Street to the apartment just before the murder. The passenger, a very large middle-aged woman, had asked him to wait for her to return but never came back. The police took the driver on a stakeout of the Dornblaser home, where he positively identified the woman as the one he had delivered to the scene. She was arrested later that day and, after six hours of interrogation, confessed to the brutal killing.

The call she placed to Seymer just before the murder was not only about receipts and leaking coils. In recent weeks, Dornblaser had been adamant that Seymer pay to have her apartment redecorated. Seymer was adamant in refusing. The day of the murder she asked yet again, and Seymer again refused, telling her that if she did not like it, she could move. "I'm coming to see you," Dornblaser spat before hanging up the phone. Fifteen minutes later, the argument continued in Seymer's front room. "I just got mad," Dornblaser told police. "I slapped her several times in the face. Then I took the pipe out of my purse and I hit her. I don't remember how many times. I just kept hitting her." Shown the gloves that were stuffed into Seymer's throat, ultimately choking her to death, Dornblaser said she did not remember putting them into Seymer's mouth but admitted they were hers.

She said after the murder, she washed the blood from her hands in the bathroom and left the building through a service elevator. Not wanting to be seen, she walked downtown and took a streetcar home. Police asked if any of Seymer's blood ended up on her clothing. "Yes, there was," she cried, tugging at the hem of the thin, blue dress she wore. "This is the dress I had on. I have washed it off." After washing away Seymer's blood, Dornblaser went out to the Futuristic Ballroom at North Second and Wisconsin to play bingo, a game to which she claimed to be addicted. She played a few cards the next day, while police built their case against her. Upon completing her confession, reporters and photographers crowded around the woman as she buried her face in her hands and wept for her daughter. "I don't know why I did it. My poor baby—what will my poor baby do?"

The next month, when her case came to trial, however, Dornblaser recanted her confession. She pled insanity to the crime, saying now that she only remembered slapping Seymer. The "300 pound bingo-playing house wife," as the papers were now calling her, denied even owning the gloves that ended Seymer's life. Her husband testified that about two years prior, his wife had changed dramatically in character, becoming moody and beginning to complain of pains and mysterious noises. Of five doctors summoned by the court, two found her to be insane and three found that she was sane enough to have known right from wrong.

When called to the stand, Dornblaser gave "halting and confusing" testimony. She spoke in soft and mumbled tones, shielding her face from the jury with a quivering hand. With tears, she claimed not to be able to remember much of the incident. Asked if she gagged Seymer, she said, "If I did, I don't remember. But I don't think I did, I wouldn't do something like that." Asked if she clubbed her with the pipe, she said, "No, I wouldn't do such a thing. If I did, I must be crazy." Handed the pipe found at the scene, she was afraid to touch it and acted as though she was entirely unfamiliar with it. "I took something out of the drawer to hammer my shoe," she said. "It might have been the pipe. It was such a long time ago." She spoke of someone who was "along" with her but claimed to be alone at Seymer's apartment. "I am taking the blame, but I did not kill her," she said, refusing to elaborate except to say, "They must have threatened to harm me or I wouldn't feel this way."

After a two-week trial, it took the jury ninety-five minutes to find Dornblaser sane and guilty of second-degree murder. The next week, she was sentenced to fourteen to twenty-five years in the state prison at Taycheedah.

IN A VIOLINIST'S HANDS
August 1884

PROFESSOR WILLIAM Moebius, well-known classical violinist and music instructor, stumbled out of a Grand Avenue gambling parlor, a loaded British Bulldog revolver in his pocket and death on his mind. It was just past 2:00 p.m. on a Sunday.

As a child, Moebius had been a musical prodigy, sent to the conservatory at Dresden at age nine and touring Prussia by age fourteen. He had played in orchestras in France, Spain, and Italy. After immigrating to America, he played in New York City and led his own orchestra in Louisville before returning to tour the grand concert halls of Europe.

In 1879, he brought his wife and eight children to Milwaukee. There, he taught music and performed with the city's Bach Orchestra. But he also took to gambling in the city. A string of heavy losses had forced him into a state of horrid dejection. Nearing the foot of the Grand Avenue Bridge, he pulled the gun from his pocket and fired a single round toward the dirt. The professor was not familiar with firearms. He had purchased the weapon and a box of ammunition only an hour earlier from a West Water Street shop. The weapon was so foreign to him that he returned to the shop a few minutes later and asked the clerk if he would be so kind as to load it. From there, he hastened to Grand Avenue and played his last ten dollars. He lost.

The volley into the ground was a practice shot. Satisfied he could operate the piece, he placed it to his chest and squeezed off four shots. The gunfire drew the attention of the midday downtown traffic. A crowd had already begun to form around Moebius when some nearby police detectives placed the still-breathing, greatly stunned, and entirely unharmed professor under arrest.

The gun Moebius placed to his heart with the intention of ending his life had been filled with blanks. The clerk who had sold Moebius the pistol was so disturbed by the professor's peculiar behavior in his shop that he had pocketed the bullets Moebius had purchased and loaded the gun with harmless imitation ammunition.

At the station, Moebius said he appreciated the clerk's deception, and that he was glad to be alive. He also expressed concern over a small bundle of letters he had dropped in a mailbox just before his failed suicide. They were addressed to various family members and friends, explaining his plight and detailing his intention of self-murder. Before his wife collected him at the station, he asked if anything could be done to prevent the letters from being delivered. He was told there was not. It was expected that the letters would be received early the next week.

"SUICIDE MANIA"
February to May 1876

O N FEBRUARY 4, 1876, sixty-four-year-old William Krall, a
basket maker, drank a half bottle of poison. Krall had long
threatened suicide. Just two weeks earlier, his wife found him
dangling by his neck from a tree branch and had cut him down.
Mrs. Krall thought she had similarly scuttled these plans when
she called a physician to their home who pumped his stomach
of the poison. But when left alone, Krall finished off the bottle,
dropping into a sleep from which he would not wake.

As was Krall, sixty-five-year-old Edward Plauschek was addicted to drink. He, too, had threatened suicide for years and,
the week after Krall's death, made good on his boast, shooting himself in his Galena Street home. The same day, Charles
Mauer, just thirty, shot himself through the head in the Union
Cemetery. He had been despondent over the recent death of his
father. The body lay at his father's grave for more than a day
before it was discovered.

Barbara Hammer was afraid for her life when she hanged
herself in the attic of her Market Street home. For months, she
had been telling anyone who would listen that her neighbors
were conspiring to murder her. The tipping point came when
she finally believed her husband to be in on the plot. It was her
husband who eventually found her, dangling from a rope tied to
the rafter with an overturned washtub at her feet.

Three weeks later, a body was recovered from the city out-
skirts, a young man with a self-directed bullet in his brain. A
young woman identified the body as that of her former lover,
Mathias Boehm. While trying to contact the father of the departed in Berton, Wisconsin, a telegram was received from
none other than Mr. Mathias Boehm. He denied shooting
himself. The *Milwaukee Sentinel* joked that the man could be
charged with perjury. The body was never identified. While the
city was still sorting out the Boehm matter, Adam Sedow was

found hanging from an oak tree on an Elizabeth Street farm. He left behind a large family with no means of support.

A month later, a woman was seen at the foot of Mason Street, pacing the beach as if, according the *Milwaukee Sentinel*, "possessed of a mania for rapid pedestrianism." She paid a boy fifty cents to row her out into the lake and back. On the way out, she began to sing and shout in incoherent tones. The boy became scared and tried to row back to shore, but as he turned, the woman leapt from the tiny craft. Other boaters tried to save her, but none could reach the woman in time. As the police attempted to recover her body with grappling hooks, a large crowd gathered on the beach. Among them was the mother of the victim, later identified as thirty-year-old Mary Daily. Mrs. Daily had a suspicion upon arriving at the scene that it was her daughter the lake held. She told police that Mary had been subject to psychotic fits since the age of nine and was prone to drunkenness.

Four days after Daily drowned herself, police arrested a man named Fritz Frowitz on suspicion of possessing stolen goods. Frowitz was better known as the Red Butcher due to his bright orange hair and occasional profession. The butcher was also a known petty thief and drunk and was in his typical stupor when pinched. Still in his boozy haze, he hanged himself in his jail cell. The two stolen items he was accused of possessing were a woman's shawl and a photo album.

The next week, a man named Peter Brecker shot himself after being diagnosed as an "incurable." Three days later, Amelia Bolkenius drowned herself off of South Point. Bolkenius had been declared insane some forty years earlier and was under the constant watch of her family. In an unguarded moment, she stole away and made haste to the lake.

On May 18, just months after being discharged from an insane asylum, James Frawley ended his life with a pistol shot to the brain. He committed the deed in the bedroom of his family home on Eighth Street. His wife was in the next room and his two small children were in school at the time. Ten days later,

Elizabeth Braasch wandered into a gravel pit behind her home and lay in a puddle that was no more than a foot deep, keeping her face submerged until she was no longer of this mortal coil. The next day, Johnny Farrell fired a single shot at his mother-in-law, whom he blamed for the recent breakup of his marriage. His first shot missed, but his second, aimed at his own temple, met its mark. In lieu of a note explaining his actions, he left a short poem, blaming his troubles on love.

On May 31, the *Milwaukee Sentinel* reported the death of twenty-eight-year-old Christina Kindling under the headline THE SUICIDE MANIA. "Every day," the paper wrote, "witnesses a violation of 'the cannon 'gainst self-slaughter.'" Kindling had arisen as usual on her final morning. She began to fix breakfast for her husband, Herman, who sat in the next room of their little Reed Street duplex. Her daughters, ages two and three, were still asleep. Days earlier, she had confessed to Herman that she had carried on an affair with a neighbor during her husband's recent jail term. He agreed to an amicable separation, but the pending disgrace was too much for Christina. A dreadful scream jolted Herman from his paper. He hastened to the kitchen and found Christina, seated in a chair, with her throat split open. A bloody carving knife lay nearby. She had run the blade across her neck twice, ear to ear and back again, with enough force to completely sever her windpipe.

With the horrific demise of Christina Kindling, Milwaukee's "suicide mania" ebbed. At least fifteen suicides occurred during the troubled four-month stretch—an unlikely proportion of the reported total of twenty-five for the year.

MRS. KRIMMER'S SON
August 1881

H ERMAN HILDEN was unaware that his mother, Louisa, was married to Paul Krimmer when he paid the couple a visit at their south-side tavern, but he knew of their relationship.

Indeed, most of Milwaukee knew of the relationship, thanks to the scandal it had caused just a year earlier. Louisa was still married to Sebastian Hilden, Herman's father, when she met and took up with Krimmer, a schoolteacher whose wife had recently passed away. The Hilden divorce was gossiped about breathlessly, costing Krimmer his job and driving Sebastian to flee to St. Louis with Herman. Herman had not seen his mother in more than a year when he entered her barroom and introduced himself to Krimmer.

Louisa wept when her husband told her that her son wished to see her. Herman's disapproval of her relationship with Krimmer bordered on mania. Just seventeen years old but appearing even younger, the boy had once already tried to kill his mother. Another time, in a fit of depression, he turned a gun on himself, plugging a single bullet into his chest. But such history did not overwhelm the bounds of family, and Louisa set a table for her son and husband and poured a round of drinks.

In St. Louis, Herman had taken up his father's habit of over-indulging with the bottle and absorbed every bit of anger that festered inside the elder Hilden for his wife. The Hildens had been married in Germany, where Sebastian made a good living as a wool spinner. He first suspected his wife of infidelity in the old country, saying later that she was "very much given to flirtations with other men." For reasons not given, Louisa fled the situation in Germany, abruptly packing up her children and whisking them across the Atlantic while Sebastian was out of the country. It was months before he was able to join them, steaming across the Atlantic and into Milwaukee, where Louisa had eventually settled. There, he felt duty-bound to reunite the family he accused her of trying to ruin. It was shortly thereafter that she met Krimmer.

As mother and son caught up over drinks, the conversation in the tavern was light and pleasant. But when Louisa turned the discussion toward weightier topics, her son bristled. She asked if the wound in his chest gave him much trouble. "Only in warm weather," he replied. She asked him if he was still drinking as much as he used to. "Yes," he replied with a snort. At that, Herman arose and declared himself ready for bed. He reached into his breast pocket, as if to look for a billfold, and asked how much he owed for the drinks. Krimmer replied that there would be no charge. As Herman insisted, his mother noticed something in his pocket with a long, white handle. She asked him was it was. "Nothing dangerous," Herman answered as he removed the object, a pearl-handled revolver, and aimed it squarely at his mother's chest. He fired once, tearing a hole through her ribs and sending her flailing to the floor. Krimmer leapt up in terror, but he was already in Herman's sights. A single shot to the heart sent him tumbling backward.

"Oh, Herman!" his mother cried as he hastened across the bloody floor toward the exit. "What have you done?" She managed to pull herself to her husband and took him in her arms. "Pa!" she wailed. "Is it as bad as all that?" The man's only reply came as a blood-choked gurgle. Minutes later, he was dead.

As his stepfather died in his mother's lap, Herman jumped on a streetcar and rode to a tavern at Fourteenth and Cherry Streets where he met an old friend. After a round of drinks, the boy admitted what he had done. The friend convinced Herman to head to another bar, where a policeman they knew was having a drink. After recounting his story, he went with the officer to a nearby police station. Inside, he laid down his pistol and confessed.

Despite the seemingly open-and-shut nature of the case, the saga of Herman Hilden was far from complete. He went to trial seven months later and pled not guilty by reason of insanity. The jury hung itself, seven voting for acquittal and five for the penitentiary. While awaiting retrial, Hilden escaped by locking a guard in a furnace room and fleeing through an open door. The escape was part of a plan hatched by him and his cell mates one evening after a sympathetic jailer allowed them a bottle of whiskey. Hilden was supposed to brain the guard with a fire poker, steal his keys, and free the entire prison population, but he lost his nerve and ran. He made it as far as Appleton before wiring the Milwaukee sheriff, asking for someone to come get him and take him home to his cell.

While awaiting his retrial, Hilden became a wealthy man. A relative in Germany passed away, leaving the young man a small fortune. Even as he was unable to enjoy the fruits of his windfall, Hilden was a model prisoner after his abortive escape. His father and siblings visited him regularly. His mother, now remarried and living in Chicago, refused to visit, even declining to testify at his trial.

In March 1883, a jury reached a peculiar verdict in the case, finding Hilden to have been insane at the time of his crime, but presently of sound mind. The declaration freed Hilden of any responsibility for the murder and forbade the state to continue to hold him as a potential threat. Once mad but now cured in the eyes of the law, Herman Hilden was set free and given his fortune. He was still just twenty years old.

ODORS
March 1876

J OSEPHINE WILLNER, a woman of about forty years, trim and displaying a fading beauty, was surrounded by enemies. They had murdered her husband, her father, and her brother. They had chased her from Milwaukee, followed her to Ohio, and even pursued her across the ocean on her European vacations. She was certain they meant to end her life.

Some of these enemies were human, but others were in the form of "medicated odors." The odors found her everywhere—they clouded her home, lay in her bed, and penetrated her food. And there were doctors behind it all. A small clutch of Milwaukee physicians, she believed, meant to do away with her. Finally, at wit's end, she purchased a pistol and set out to defend herself.

Abraham Willner, Josephine's husband, had died in 1873 under mysterious circumstances, taking ill shortly after their marriage and quickly passing away. His doctors believed he might have been poisoned. When Josephine suddenly became wealthy after his death, rumors flew that she was the beneficiary of a substantial life insurance policy. She insisted her fortune was an inheritance.

As a widow, Willner began to behave strangely. She rarely slept and was known to wander the streets at night. She was often agitated and impulsive, engaging in numerous sexual encounters and partaking "in a thousand queer whims and impossible fancies." But perhaps most notably, she became extremely paranoid about doctors. She ranted about certain Milwaukee doctors who were attempting to kill her. Fearful for her life, she left the city and moved back to her birthplace of Geneva, Ohio.

Willner became particularly fixated on Dr. John E. Garner, a highly respected and well-established Milwaukee physician. She blamed Garner for the death of her husband, then those of her brother, father, and cousin. Willner herself admitted that Garner had not treated any of the departed. She did, however, claim to have been treated by Garner herself, saying that he had diagnosed her with "female weakness" and had filled her with "horrible drugs and stinking medicine." Asked for specifics about her illness, she demurred, replying, "Oh, I can't tell you. It's too vulgar."

In 1875, Willner visited friends and family in Milwaukee. Even during her short visit, her behavior frightened her loved ones. If they found her to be acting strangely in the wake of her husband's death, they now thought her absolutely mad. Family members planned to confront her on the matter, but she fled before they had a chance. In the spring of 1876, she bought a gun, a nickel-plated five-ball Wesson and Harrington. The torment of her enemies had become too much to bear.

On March 2, Willner rode the Chicago and North Western line from Ashtabula, Ohio, to Milwaukee. She arrived in the city around 8:30 p.m., hired a hack at the lakefront depot, and instructed the driver to take her to Dr. Garner's home at 464

Jefferson Street. Willner was highly agitated during the short ride. Arriving at the doctor's house, she instructed the driver to wait, and slowly made her way to the front door. She rang the bell and Dr. Garner's daughter answered. Willner asked for the girl's father and the daughter called for him. He approached the door, and without a word between them, Willner pulled out her pistol and shot him in the chest. "My God!" he exclaimed, falling to the floor, "I'm shot!"

Willner walked back to the hack as calmly as she had climbed the stairs and asked the driver to take her the Newhall House, where she planned to stay. The driver was terrified over what he had just witnessed and obeyed her in a near trance. As they pulled away, Garner's family gathered in horror around the dying man.

The driver took off in a tear toward the hotel, but approaching downtown, Willner called at him to instead go to the law offices of Finches, Lynde & Miller. He did so and waited pensively as she tried the front door. It was locked, and she returned to the carriage and said she wished to go to the hotel. The driver started out, but again she called to him to reroute. Now, she wanted to be dropped at the home of Dr. Spearman, another Milwaukee physician whom she suspected of plotting against her. But again, after changing course, she stopped him. To the Newhall, she again told the wearied man. He beat there in a flash and quickly deposited his passenger, no doubt thrilled to be rid of her company.

At the Newhall, Willner registered under her own name and took a late supper. About twenty minutes after she went to her room, police officers knocked on her door. With a small crowd of gawkers looking on, Willner was placed under arrest for the shooting of Garner. "Oh, I meant to do it," she told a detective. "I couldn't help it. He killed my husband, father, uncle, and brother and has made my life a torment. I did it in self-defense. I had to defend myself, for he sent them to follow me everywhere." She made no resistance to her arrest but objected strongly when police seized her pistol. She needed it still, she claimed, as there may be others who wanted her dead.

From the hotel, Willner was taken back to the Garner home, where the wounded doctor lay dying in a second-floor bedroom. After being positively identified by several people there, she was whisked to the central station, where an even larger group had formed as the news of Dr. Garner's bizarre assault had spread.

The next day, a *Milwaukee Sentinel* reporter interviewed her in her cell. Willner "was dressed in deep mourning and wore a heavy black veil." Her hair was done neatly in black curls and her eyes beamed a stunning blue. She "must have been beautiful in her youth," the paper noted. When informed that the doctor had died, she was unmoved. "I am glad of it," she said. "That is what I came here for. Oh! I couldn't stand it any longer. He made my life a torment. Wherever I went he followed."

Two months later, Willner pled not guilty to the murder by reason of insanity. She was initially found to be sane and given a sentence of life, but this verdict was thrown out on appeal. A retrial found her to be insane and she was sent to the women's asylum at Oshkosh, where she would spend the rest of her days in the constant company of doctors.

"BLOOD ENDS A FEUD"
April 1895

PATROLMAN D. J. O'Connell was walking his Sunday night beat along a fashionable stretch of Grand Avenue when he recognized a figure staggering toward him through the calm evening air. The man, under the influence but not in a stupor, was Emil Sanger. O'Connell knew Sanger, a prominent if not somewhat disagreeable character, and urged him to head for home. Sanger refused, saying that he was out to find his wife, whom he thought to be at the home of Sam Luscombe, her father, which stood within sight of where the two men talked.

O'Connell knew there was a feud between Sanger and his wife's family. Sanger's agitated state told O'Connell that there might be trouble. He searched the man for weapons and, finding none, let him pass. Sanger marched across the grass of the Luscombe home to a side door, where he pounded and demanded entry. While O'Connell lingered on the sidewalk, Sanger called back to him. "Come up here, I want to speak to you."

"Come here if you want to speak to me," O'Connell answered. Just then, a curtain behind a plate-glass window in the door lifted. Seconds later, a shotgun blast shattered the evening calm. Sanger reeled back and fell dead to the pavement, his face torn apart by the twin-barreled weapon. O'Connell called to his nearby partner to fetch more officers and a doctor. The side door opened and a man in a long coat emerged. He called out to O'Connell, saying that his name was Robert Luscombe. "I am the man who did it," he continued. "I want to go to the central station and give myself up."

The gunman and the deceased had a history. Emil Sanger was the son of Casper Sanger, one of Milwaukee's most prominent practitioners in matters both financial and political. His firms employed hundreds, and he had served in several elected capacities. Robert Luscombe had been employed for years within the Sanger empire, working side-by-side with Emil until Luscombe left the city to study law. By 1886, both young men were prospering, Sanger running a silver mine in California, and Luscombe back in Milwaukee, serving as a city attorney.

But a silver panic in the early 1890s wiped out the Sanger interests in the west. When Emil returned to the city, he was broke but not alone. In California, he had won the affections of his bookkeeper's wife, and in 1892, he married the woman—the former Nellie Luscombe, Robert's sister. Although Sanger and Luscombe were now kin, the relationship between the two families—and particularly between Emil and Robert—quickly eroded. His money troubles growing, Sanger began to drink heavily, irrationally pinning all his miseries on the mild-mannered and affable Luscombe. At home, he laid his rage on Nellie, beating her regularly. He once chased her from their home with a loaded pistol, cursing her as she hid in a nearby barn.

Sanger made no attempt to hide his hatred for Luscombe. He told several people, including Samuel S. Barney, a newly elected member of the US Congress, that he planned to kill Luscombe on sight. Few took these hot-tempered threats—made both drunken and sober—with any real concern. After Sanger damned Luscombe's name in a downtown saloon one afternoon, a group of men who knew Luscombe spoke up. "Bob's a friend of mine and I think he's all right," said one man. "He's a dashed good fellow," added another.

Sanger approached the group. "My card, sir," he said to one of Luscombe's defenders, handing him his calling card. "You will have to answer to me for that remark, sir. I demand that you meet me and fight a duel!" The men all laughed heartily at the gesture and Sanger stormed from the hall in a fury.

But to his wife, Sanger's threats were deadly serious. He took to wearing a gun belt, telling Nellie he planned to use it to shoot down that "damned brother of yours!" The Friday before his death, Sanger had gone to Luscombe's house with the intention of shooting him dead in his doorway but found that no one was home. Returning to his house, he savagely beat Nellie with closed fists and a buggy whip. "Damn you!" he screamed. "You look like your brother!" She attempted to flee, but Sanger had locked every door in the house in anticipation of the attack. Finally, he showed her a knife and threatened to kill her if she ever tried to leave him. The next day, with Sanger out of the house, Nellie fled to her father's house. She was so badly beaten he did not even recognize her. After calling for a doctor, he dashed off a note to his son. "Nell is here all battered to pieces," it read. "Come immediately, armed for an emergency."

Luscombe claimed the shot he unloaded at point-blank range into Sanger's face was an act of self-defense. He feared that Sanger was about to break down the door, kill him, and then finish off his sister. But while Sanger was certainly agitated, there was no indication he was about to break through the door or the window. And despite the numerous threats against Luscombe, Sanger was unarmed when he was shot, and indeed might not have even known that Luscombe was inside the house.

In July 1895, Luscombe went to trial. The salacious details of the case, as well as the prominence of the two families involved, made it perhaps the most famous murder case the city had yet seen. The trial lasted most of the month, but a verdict was brought in just ten minutes. Luscombe, eminently polite and likeable, was found not guilty for doing away with Sanger, a man for whom few tears were shed. Writing that the dead man had often been called a brute, the *Milwaukee Journal* retorted, "To compare [Sanger] to the lower animals of creation was a libel on the brute."

"HE MIGHT HAVE KNOWN..."
October 1852

O N A chilly October morning, a group of about twenty people gathered around the front windows of the I. A. Hopkins bookstore near the corner of Wisconsin and Water Streets, gawking at a collection of caricatures the shop was displaying. Across the street, watching the watchers, twenty-six-year-old Mary Ann Wheeler stood outside of the lodging house in which she rented a small basement room. She pulled her shawl up around her shoulders and crossed the street. Among the gapers was John M. W. Lace, a theater usher and part-time fire company member. As she strode briskly across the cobblestone street, Wheeler drew a double-barreled pistol from a pocket in her dress. Stepping atop the wooden-plank sidewalk, she placed the gun to the back of Lace's neck and pulled the trigger.

The dual shots crackled in a terrifying report that scattered bystanders from the scene and tore a gruesome fissure through the base of Lace's skull. He crumbled into a lifeless heap as a crimson stream of blood sprayed from the wound. "I have done what I meant to do and to do it publically," Wheeler declared to a gaggle of stunned onlookers. A sheriff's deputy quickly arrived on the scene, to whom Wheeler presented her pistol. "You can have it," she told him plainly. "I am willing. I have killed John Lace and am proud of it. I'll go with you wherever you like."

Wheeler was born in Clarksfield, Ohio, in 1826, the daughter of "poor, yet respectable" parents. She left home for reasons unknown at age twenty and settled in Milwaukee three years later. She found work as milliner, sewing women's bonnets in a small downtown factory. She enrolled at dancing school but left after "certain persons made reports prejudicial to her character." Bouts of depression overwhelmed her, and she was often sick and unable to eat. She took to smoking opium and was occasionally observed by her landlady, Miss Cleveland, "waltzing alone" in her room.

In 1851, after separating from his wife, Lace moved into the same rooming house as Wheeler and took an immediate interest in his pretty young neighbor. Miss Cleveland warned her to keep away from the rakish Lace. But he was kind to Wheeler when few others were. He assured her that they would be wed after his divorce was finalized. Wheeler fell for his charms and the pair engaged in a torrid affair.

But when Wheeler became pregnant, Lace ended the relationship. He told her he wanted nothing to do with her or their child. Wheeler wrote him constantly, begging him for money to use for an abortion. She threatened to have the child and tarnish him with scandal if he did not finance the procedure. He refused and was known to read her pitiful letters aloud to his grog house pals, boasting of the lovesick and broken condition in which he had left her. He told his bar mates that Wheeler was a common whore and that if they "wanted something," all they need do was bring a few coins to her room.

The jolt of Lace's sudden and cruel rejection was a crippling blow to an already unsound mind. Wheeler managed to raise the money to have the pregnancy terminated, but the emotional effects of the affair would not be so easily put away. Wheeler lost all interest in her personal well-being. She became short with housemates and coworkers and developed a strange and volatile temper. She tried suicide with arsenic and was found on various occasions beating her head or fists against the walls of her boarding room. She told anyone who would listen of her desire to die. Her prayers turned to curses at God for allowing her to keep living.

In early September 1852, she bought a pistol. She told the merchant who sold her the weapon that she was going to be traveling and wanted something for protection. The man even sawed the barrels short so it could fit inside a pocket on her dress. Wheeler made no secret of the gun. One acquaintance later told police she would take it from her pocket "as lightly as she would show a picture." She used it at least once before the killing of Lace, chasing another woman while firing wildly at her feet and cackling madly at her terror. Just days before the killing, she also acquired a large knife and took to arming herself at all times.

Her manic behavior of the preceding year belied the relatively calm way in which she conducted herself upon her arrest. When asked at the scene why she had shot Lace, she replied, "I don't wish to answer those questions now. I will do so at a proper time." As her story came out, Lace was portrayed in the newspapers as the dastardly "seducer" of the poor, young Wheeler. Those who knew him well found it difficult to defend the deceased. Wheeler herself never denied that she intended to kill Lace, nor did she express any sorrow. Her only regret was that he had died so suddenly. "He might have known," she told police, "by whose hand he died."

Wheeler went to trial in May 1853. That she killed Lace was not in doubt. The issue to be settled was whether or not Wheeler was sane at the time of the murder. Her defense team argued that Lace was no victim at all but rather a "seducer— that worst of robbers because he plunders happiness; that worst of murderers because he murders innocence." They further claimed her actions to be not merely those of an insane person but of one whose madness was of divine origin. "It was so ordained that the very wrongs she endured at the hand [of Lace]," her defense told the court, "should so work upon her mind as to make her an instrument in the hand of Almighty God to punish her seducer and to rid the world of a monster."

The jury was out for three days, deliberating day and night, but returned without a verdict. Wheeler went on trial again the next month and on June 4, 1853, was found not guilty by reason of temporary insanity. With that, Mary Ann Wheeler was set free. The next morning, it was reported, Wheeler rented the finest carriage to be had in the city and "was driven around the streets like a heroine."

ACCIDENTS

A PLACE CANNOT grow from settlement to city to metropolis without the occasional loss of innocents during its great march forward. The bystanders left broken and buried in nascent Milwaukee were victims of both fate and chance. As the little village by the lake expanded, the chances for large-scale disaster multiplied, answering to the sometimes terrible arithmetic of progress. Fire consumed wooden palaces, the seas claimed the ships built to tame them, and the iron, brick, and mud of an altered landscape struck back against its populace. Some of these tragedies might have been avoided, others seemed inevitable, but none were acts of malice or evil. They were not as much things that were done as they were things that simply happened.

While these accidents give the appearance of a feckless brand of destiny, they often were bred of common problems and occasionally led to useful—if not untimely—solutions. And, as it does today, the city demands to know *why* when its citizens are broken, maimed, or killed. But, as the crowds that descended immediately upon the sites of these great tragedies, often thousands deep, gawking and straining to see for themselves the unfortunates of the latest awful act of God, the why was never quite so pressing as the more visceral and forbidden *how*.

While these accidents and tragedies leave a tangible legacy today in various laws, codes, and regulations, it is the hidden remnants of these events that link us most closely with the pitiable lost of these stories. And while we pass these places every day without a second thought as to their gruesome pasts, the city remembers the crowds who once flocked to pay witness.

The masses have long gone from these sites, but they remain watched, the ghosts of eyes who could not turn away.

❖   ❖   ❖

"A PITILESS WORLD"
October 1882

M AGGIE HENNECKE rode to school in the family carriage, dressed neatly in a navy suit with a turn-down collar, a straw hat, and high-buttoned boots. Maggie was the twelve-year-old daughter of C. H. Hennecke, a Milwaukeean prominent in both business and civic affairs. The carriage deposited Maggie and her five siblings at the German-American Academy School on North Broadway. As each of the Hennecke children set off for their classrooms, nothing in Maggie's temperament seemed amiss. During the lunch hour, she appeared to be happy and gave no indication of trouble. But after lunch, Maggie did not return to class. Early that afternoon, a girl matching her description was spotted on Cass Street, a few blocks east of her school, sitting at a street corner and crying. A coach operator approached the girl and asked what the trouble was. She said nothing, only jumped up and ran away. Two more sightings of the girl just south of the Milwaukee River suggested she might have been walking back to the family home at 318 Hanover Street. She would never get there.

It was two days before the family went public with Maggie's disappearance. The search for the girl was intensive from the outset. The family discounted rumors that she had suffered from a "temporary aberration of the mind" and insisted that she had been kidnapped. Her father offered a two-thousand-dollar reward for her safe return. The only tangible clue to the disappearance was Maggie's straw hat, which was found near the shores of the city's inner harbor in the days after she vanished.

The case's publicity, and the reward money offered, brought out the usual roster of cranks and cheats. Sightings of the girl and reports of various abduction plots came in from across the nation. Some who claimed to have information demanded a share of the reward money up front. The family brought in various spiritualists and mediums to locate the girl. All claimed that she was still alive. Some said she was being hidden in some sinister corner of the city. Meanwhile, acting on the belief that she might have been taken and forced into a life of prostitution, police searched each of Milwaukee's several dozen brothels for any trace of the girl.

About three weeks after she vanished, a man named George Brown, a self-proclaimed private detective from North Dakota, "arrested" two men in Lincoln, Nebraska. Brown boasted to the newspapers that the men had confessed to abducting the girl, and he found in their possession a ring that the girl was wearing when she vanished. Milwaukee authorities dismissed Brown as a lunatic and denied that the arrested men had anything to do with the case. The same newspaper accounts of the Brown arrests also recounted whisperings that Maggie was living contentedly in Minneapolis with two single men.

As the winter of 1882 gave way to the spring thaw of 1883, interest in the case of Maggie Hennecke faded. The family held out hope, keeping the two-thousand-dollar reward available, but grimly adding a two-hundred-dollar reward for anyone who could lead them to the discovery of her body. In late April, after a speeding tugboat had churned up the waters of the Kinnickinnic River, a Jones Island seaman spotted the tiny body, still dressed in blue, near the foot of National Avenue. As word of the finding spread, crowds gathered at the spot. With no trauma to the body, the prevailing theory was that the girl had lost her hat near the river and fallen in and drowned trying to retrieve it. Dredging in the area and the regular traffic of steamboats could have pulled the body deep under the water, trapping it until the spring boat passages knocked it loose. In reflecting on the case, the burst of opportunism it inspired, and its slow and sad fade from the public awareness, the *Milwaukee Sentinel* expressed relief that the girl was at peace. "Better so," the paper wrote, "than alive at the mercy of a pitiless world."

MISFIRE

July 1880

MARY VAN Avery had been employed at the Hanley Saloon and Boarding House on Ferry Street just two weeks when she brought her daughter with her to work. The girl, two-year-old Mamie, had until recently been in the care of her grandmother. Young Mamie, who was sometimes known with a last name of Shea, was rumored to have been the illegitimate child of a prominent Milwaukee businessman. Mary had shown so little interest in the girl that the grandmother had made at least one attempt to have the child committed to a Catholic orphanage. Finally, she told Mary that if she did not come to claim Mamie, she was going to turn her loose to wander wherever she may. Mary retrieved the girl on the Fourth of July and took her to the Ferry Street saloon the next day.

The saloon was situated within sight of the various piers and docks near where the Milwaukee River met the Menomonee River. It was operated by Captain Pat Henley, who himself had a small child, eight-year-old Georgie. As Mary went about her job duties with Mamie in tow, Georgie watched the other boys of the neighborhood with jealousy as they set off firecrackers and small shells left over from the previous day's celebration. Using a dollar he raised from selling a goat, Georgie walked to the south-side junk shop of D. S. Lederer and purchased an old breech-loading pistol. At the neighboring shop of gunmaker John Meunier, he bought a box of .22-caliber balls.

Back at the saloon, Georgie and his friends tried in every way to get the wretched old gun to fire. But the hammer was too weak to ignite the charge. Georgie found Mary in the kitchen, where she was scrubbing dishes with Mamie at her feet. He aimed the piece at the door and tried a few more times in vain to fire it, commenting to Mary that he could be arrested for playing with such an item. Convinced the pistol would never fire and having no interest in it as a mere accessory, he turned to Mary and asked if she could return it for him. Mary's reply went unrecorded, but as she bent down to pick up her daughter, Georgie tried the trigger one last time. The hammer fell true and ignited the charge, propelling the ball across the room. It struck Mamie directly in the heart, just between two of her mother's outstretched fingers. The girl died within moments.

Startled by the shot and the screams of Mary, Georgie ran from the scene. He was later found hiding in the city's Third Ward. In order to stop the boy's constant wailing, police had to assure him the girl was going to survive. When he was finally told she had died, he fainted cold. Back at the scene, Mamie's grandmother was inconsolable. Newspaper accounts noted that her grief was far more visible than that of Mary. Police had to separate the two when the grandmother began to loudly berate Mary for bringing the girl to such a place.

In the days that followed, whispers were heard that suggested someone else had killed the girl and placed the blame on the boy, knowing he would never be charged with a crime. Police asked the still-shaken Georgie to load and fire the weapon to put these rumors down. At an inquest of the incident, neither man who had sold Georgie the weaponry was willing to accept any blame. "I sell on call without questioning the motives of the buyer or bothering about the consequences," said Lederer, the man who had sold Georgie the gun. Meunier, who had supplied the balls, noted there was no law against selling ammunition to children and, had he not sold to the boy, another merchant certainly would have. A grand jury hearing the case levied no charges, but issued "censure in the severest terms" to the adults involved.

THE FOURTH
July 1875

I N THE wake of a particularly gruesome Independence Day
weekend, Milwaukee police were ordered to confiscate all
pistols being used by careless celebrants of the holiday. The ca-
sualties of the Fourth were numerous: A Walnut Street man
blew away his own thumb while firing a revolver, a man in the
same neighborhood was shot in the leg by a stray bullet while
walking home, another man lost an eye when an improperly
loaded weapon exploded in his face, and yet another had his
hand mangled in a similar accident. One reveler thought it
safer to load his gun with stones, only to have the charge ignite
unexpectedly. The damage from the blast, the *Milwaukee Sentinel* noted, was likely to cripple him permanently. The paper
also noted the loss of a ten-year-old boy's thumb while the child
was "blazing away with an old revolver."

Still more accidents occurred from the careless use of firecrackers. At least one house was burned and a boy disfigured
from various explosions. The most tragic incident of the weekend, however, was the death of young Bertha Schockaert. The
girl was near her home at Vliet Street and Wells when a fire-
cracker ignited her dress. She was ablaze "from head to toe"
before a neighbor doused her with a pail of water. The girl died
the next day.

THE TEN O'CLOCK TRAIN
July 1893

A YOUNG man ran jovially about the idle cars and long ribbons of track of the Chicago and North Western Railroad's
lakefront yards. The boy, dressed plainly and wearing a me-
chanic's apron, had been a nuisance to the depot workers all

morning. Just past 10:00 a.m., a car cleaner yelled at him to get out, but the boy refused and went about his bothersome routine. Minutes later, he was found lying on the track nearest the lake, near the foot of Wisconsin Avenue. His left arm and head had been horrifically separated from his body, which was badly mangled and bruised. Officials determined that the boy had been hit by the inbound Lakeshore Line passenger train. No one witnessed the accident.

The body was taken to the morgue, where it was later identified as seventeen-year-old Anthony Paitzick. The only items found on the body were a set of tickets to the Thirteenth Ward school picnic. Paitzick, wrote the *Sentinel*, was known to be "a little demented."

SWITCHMAN
March 1892

TWO TRAINS rumbled east through the massive rail yards of the Menomonee Valley. One was the evening passenger train from Watertown. The other was the Milwaukee and St. Paul shop train. The shop train was seven cars long and filled with about three hundred railroad workmen on their way home after a day's labor. Among the twisting ribbons of iron rail was switchman Emil Barthel. It was his job to open and close the many switches linked to the tracks, allowing the massive engines to slide from track to track. But on this drowsy Tuesday evening, somewhere near the foot of North Eighteenth Street, Barthel missed one.

As the Watertown train rolled east, engineer James Little spotted the neglected switch and threw the engine into reverse, yanking the handle for the air breaks. But his action came too late. With a screeching jolt, the locomotive slid forward across the divergent track and crashed at an angle into the heart of the shop train. Both trains derailed and two shop cars tumbled onto their sides. Dozens of men leapt from the cars as they tipped. Seven were crushed to death as it fell.

As the mangled bodies were pulled from the wreck, Barthel turned himself into police. Joined by his wife and young daughter at the station, the twenty-nine-year-old was beyond consolation. He told a reporter that he preferred death himself than to have caused so much agony. His fellow workers expressed support for Barthel, calling on him in their off hours to see if he needed anything. His family stayed with him as long as they were allowed, his little girl asking the uniformed officers why "Papa" was not permitted to go home with them.

Back at the yards, the accident scene was cleaned up and the entire works were back to normal by the next morning. A railroad official said that the damage from the wreck, at first estimated as high as ten thousand dollars, would likely amount to no more than a few hundred dollars. The official also announced that the railroad would cover all costs involved in burying the dead.

An inquest the day after the accident found Barthel, as the man in charge of the fatal switch, to be responsible for the wreck. He was charged with a single count of murder and held for almost three months before standing trial. The trial lasted three days, with many coworkers testifying as to his strong character and competence on the job. Barthel testified himself, sorrowfully admitting he had left the switch open as the result of a simple mistake. It took the jury just twenty minutes to return a verdict of not guilty.

COLLAPSE

March 1876

THE MILWAUKEE, Lake Shore, and Western Railroad freighter, headed by the locomotive *Idaho*, was more than two hours late as it chugged slowly along the northbound tracks past Juneau Park. A storm had battered the city the day before, soaking the recently thawed earth and then coating it in ice as temperatures dropped. Crews had worked through the morning to melt the ice from the tracks, causing the long delay, but they failed to notice the loosened soil beneath the right-of-way. Along the park, the tracks ran atop a ten-foot bluff, which was—after the extreme weather of the day before—waterlogged and coated in ice. As the steam engine *Idaho* roared past the park, the ground beneath the track gave out, dropping the engine, its three cars, and sixty feet worth of bluff into the thrashing lakefront. The train's engineer and fireman were killed in the fall, their bodies pinned beneath the wreckage. As word of the collapse spread, thousands pressed their way into the park to peer over the land's edge, down at the terrible scene below. The bodies of the dead were plainly visible in between the crashing lake waves. The *Milwaukee Sentinel* reported that the fireman, John Lynch, had his head so badly mangled in the crash that the coroner had to reshape it before allowing the body to be viewed.

Happier times along the rails in Juneau Park
WHi Image ID 47512

FIRE IN THE SKY
October 1929

I T WAS Fire Prevention Week when a patrolman on his downtown beat looked up at City Hall and noticed a twinkling
wreath of light ringing the glass dome of the building's clock
tower. The officer assumed the glowing lights to be a clever
part of the fire department's display on fire prevention at the
hall. But when the lights began pulsating and crawling toward
the very peak of the tower—nearly four hundred feet above
the sidewalk—it became clear that this was no promotion. The
city's landmark structure was burning.

Fire companies were quickly summoned to the scene. With
City Hall's famous clock stopped dead at 7:07, stiff winds blew
debris from a temporary scaffolding set up around the tower
and into the streets. That day, crews had been working to re-
place the flagpole atop the building. It was a spark from the
welding of the new pole that had hidden itself somewhere in the
tower, smoldering for hours before bursting into flames. The
winds showered cinders from the blaze and stoked the flames
into a menacing burst that taunted the chill fall air. Firemen
extinguished the cinders as they fell and soaked a number of
small fires that sprung up in the area around the tower but
were unable to do anything at all about the fire in the sky. City
Hall was not equipped with the pumps needed to get streams
of water to such a high point, nor was the fire department ca-
pable of generating the force to thrust streams to the top of the
state's tallest building. As 150 firemen stood helpless in the
streets below, the whipping winds pulled and teased the flames,
presenting a ghastly image for the thousands who gathered beneath to watch. What they saw, the *Milwaukee Journal* wrote,
was "like a bride crowned with a fiery wreath with a train of
sparks behind."

After nearly an hour on the scene, fire companies decided to
attempt to use the powerful pumps of the department's fireboat

Torrent. The vessel docked at the Kilbourn Street bridge and hundreds of feet of hose were laid through the street. As a dozen firemen worked at hoisting the hose up the side of the tower, another crew worked on the reachable floors of the building, soaking the place to its core to prevent the fire from spreading downward. The crew worked with diligence, as some observers feared that the clock tower, in its weakened state, could drop City Hall's bell, the ten-ton *Solomon Juneau*, through the southern end of the building in a terrible gash of destruction. By the time the hose had been raised the twelve floors to City Hall's peak, the great distance between the pump and the nozzle resulted in a pathetic mist of water that did little to help the situation. "The effect," the *Journal* observed, "was more or less ludicrous."

With the lower floors guarded and the area cleared of people, all the fire companies could do was wait. Finally, about 9:00 p.m., the fire consumed all that it could at the peak of the tower and burned itself out. By midnight, the fire department had declared the scene—and the mighty *Solomon Juneau*—to be secure.

FIRE WILD
August 1854

NO ONE noticed as a spark took hold at high noon at the Davis Livery Stable, located just to the rear of the US Hotel on Main Street.[1] The roof of the little tinderbox structure erupted in flames within minutes, sending a nasty plume of gray smoke into the summer sky and sounding fire bells in all corners of the city. Volunteer companies were still scrambling to the scene as the flames agitated the nearby Tremont House stables into a similar state. As the first streams of water were set upon the blaze, northerly winds fed the fire and pushed it to

---

1. Now Broadway

a series of wood-frame storefronts on East Water Street, dried and brittle from six weeks of drought and relentless sunshine. Within an hour, the entire block—Main to Water and Michigan to Huron[1]—was one nearly continuous state of conflagration.

The bulk of the city's volunteer force battled the inferno with little effect. Thick smoke held back the force's advances, and roaring bursts of heat and flame threatened their lives and gear. Several times, the men were forced to turn their hoses on themselves to prevent being overcome by the heat. One company was forced to push its hand engine into the river to avoid losing it to the fire. At 1:30, Mayor Byron Kilbourn wired to Racine for reinforcements. By the time the two hundred burly Raciners arrived, the block where the fire started had been reduced to ash and the unforgiving winds had spread the trouble as far west as the Milwaukee River. A great cheer went up from the thousands gathered around to watch the action as the Racine men joined in the fight. To aid their efforts, local officials passed out beer and whiskey by the pailful.

As the wild day grew longer, a general feeling of chaos began to overtake the scene. At 4:00 p.m., a drunken German fell from a boat, where he had been watching the action with his equally spirited friends. He was recovered from the water but did not survive. A scuffle on Huron Street resulted in the stabbing of an Irish fisherman. A ladder car driven at reckless speeds by a bone-weary member of the fire department trampled a man on Wisconsin Street. And in dozens of places, men took the disorder of the day as a chance to help themselves to the wares of various downtown merchants. More than forty men were sent to the jailhouse on charges of theft and looting—arrested by fire company members themselves as the city did not yet have a police force. As the last flames were finally soaked that night, an attempt was made on the city jail to free the men arrested that day, but the would-be rescuers were thwarted and soon made to join their compatriots under lock and key.

---

1. Now Clybourn

HORROR ON MAIN STREET
November 1869

O N A frigid November evening, a full house at the Gaiety Theatre on Main Street[1] sat rapt as a sword battle brought the house's stage melodrama to a peak. During the scene, one of the combatants accidently shattered one of the kerosene lamps that ringed the stage with a blow of his rapier. At first the mishap seemed to be a minor one. One of the actors even "playfully whisked his foot" in the small puddle of fire. But the flames quickly hit their mark, spreading across the little wooden stage and licking at the scenery and curtains. Quickly realizing the situation to be grave, the actors began to beat the flames with jackets, knocking over more lamps in the process. As members of the show urged the audience to remain calm, panic overtook the room. The exits clogged in the rush and theater-goers took to the windows, breaking out the glass and leaping into the frozen night.

The twenty-year-old house, one of the old landmarks of the city, went up with a fury in the dead winter air. As fire companies rushed to the scene, rumors spread that twenty to thirty people had been burned alive. But when the fire was tamed, just an hour after it had started, it was found that only two people from that evening's audience had not escaped. While the death toll was mercifully low, given the circumstances, recovery efforts showed the deaths to be especially horrific. Walter Brown, a middle-aged shipping clerk, was found caught behind the folding doors that led to the theater's lobby. He had been so badly burned that his flesh hung from his body in shards. Near the stage, the body of young Willie Brewer was found. Willie had worked as a newspaper apprentice. His arms had been roasted stiff, locked in front of this face, as though he had been trying to shield himself from the flames. The next morning, thousands

---

1. Now Broadway

of people filed past the site as a blustering snow covered the theater's charred shell.

DEATH'S ALLEY

October 1913

N O ONE noticed that a fire had started in an unoccupied building near the Goodyear Rubber factory on East Water Street between Wisconsin Avenue and Michigan Street. The flames had already reached the top floor of the building when an Irish setter named Scamp started to bark at the hissing flames. Scamp's owner, John Gallagher, turned in the first fire alarm at 7:30 p.m.

As the first fire companies arrived on the scene, the fire had crawled up an elevator shaft in the rear of the building and was quickly spreading to neighboring structures. Whipping winds threatened to set the entire block up in flames. Within ten minutes, twenty-two streams of water were aimed on the blaze, which shot from a dozen windows with such a hellish ferocity that it lit the evening sky as though it were high noon. "She was going like the devil," fireman Frank Komos later said.

But the fast response by city fire companies quickly had the flames under control. The roasted rubber products from the Goodyear works gave off a great stink, and heavy billows of black smoke poured from the heart of the blaze, but by 8:00 p.m., it seemed that the worst of the incident was passed. For three minutes, the scene was calm. A dozen firemen gathered in the rear alley of the building stood for an idle moment, awaiting their next orders. Charles Newton was one of them. He was about to collect his gear when he saw the rear wall of the building bulge outward. An instant later, a massive explosion blew apart the back end of the building, dropping the entire structure onto Newton and the other men. With the blast, a terrific pillar of flames shot high in the sky, raining bricks, glass, and debris over the entire block. As glass tinkled from shattered windows for hundreds of feet in every direction, firemen rushed to the back alley scene, aghast at the four feet of ruins that now covered their comrades.

Streams of water were set upon the smoldering pile. While rescuers struggled to find survivors, Reverend Francis Murphy of St. John's Church was summoned to the scene. The reverend crawled as deeply into the wreckage as he could, performing last rites for at least six men as they lay trapped, unconscious and dying. One man he was unable to reach was Charles Newton, who had been buried deep inside the mess but had not lost consciousness. Despite his precarious state, Newton would not call for help. He did not want his fellow firefighters to rush in saving him and risk missing a man more seriously injured. "It was an awful feeling," he said later, "being buried so that I couldn't move a muscle. I was not afraid of the fire, but I thought I might be covered in water and drowned if they had too bad a fire somewhere out there above me."

As the hours passed, hopes faded that any of the buried men would be recovered. Newton, as he quietly awaited the help of his comrades, heard a crew of men removing the debris from above him. As they came nearer, they spoke about the impossible odds of finding anyone still alive. "Then I felt that I could almost laugh," Newton recalled. It was past 11:00 p.m., three hours since the blast, when Newton finally called out. "Help me, boys," he said. "I am still alive.... Keep working hard and I will come out all right." Newton was covered in dirt and blood as he was pulled from the wreckage. Moments after being freed, he collapsed and was rushed to the hospital.

An inquest into the disaster in the following weeks could find no certain explanation for the explosion. Theories abounded that a fireworks firm had left behind a stock of explosives, which had been detonated in the fire. A science professor from Marquette University speculated that a quantity of rubber, which had combusted after a long exposure to heat, had done it. Yet others felt that improperly stored blasting caps were the culprit. Whatever the cause, seven dead men were pulled from the ruins of the Goodyear works that night and two more would later die of their injuries. August Pagel, in his fifth month on the job, lingered unconscious for a week before dying of injuries sustained in the blast. Charles Newton, who was able to so vividly describe his harrowing story to the newspapers the morning after the explosion, had been doomed from the moment he was blown away from the bulging back wall of the plant. He died a little more than twenty-four hours later from lacerations to his brain and a fractured skull. His wife and children were at his bedside as he passed away. He did not cry. "Good-bye dearest," he told his wife in his last moments. "Kiss me once more for the children and tell them to pray for me."

HELL PIT AT THE DAVIDSON
April 1894

A S POLICE and staff members went through the Davidson Hotel early one morning, knocking on doors and informing the seventy or so guests that the building was on fire, there did not seem to be any immediate danger. A passing beat cop had noticed gray smoke pluming from the North Third Street hotel's roof just past 4:00 a.m. But as companies arrived on the scene, they determined the fire was contained within the unoccupied Davidson Theatre, which was built into the hotel but separated from it by a thick fire wall. As the guests were informed about the situation, they dressed, collected their things, and headed out into the cool spring night.

Those in the most immediate danger seemed to be the various kitchen workers and servant girls, who were quartered above the auditorium. Also asleep above the flames was the dwarf acting troupe The Lilliputians, which was playing in the house's stage production *A Trip to Mars*. The kitchen staff and actors were hustled from the building as the fire companies began to arrive. The firemen concentrated themselves in an area near the kitchen, directly above the theater's auditorium. Beneath them, workers were busy covering the seating areas of the house with tarpaulins. The building was just four years old and the insurance company that held the theater's policy had ordered its own men to the scene to try to keep claims on the fire to a minimum. As hundreds of gallons of water were dumped into the building, it seemed that the biggest threat from the fire was to the neatly trimmed chairs and lush carpets of the auditorium.

The rebuilt Davidson Theatre and Hotel, boasting itself as "Absolutely Fire Proof," ca. 1900
WHi Image ID 53182

Around 5:00 a.m., a narrow beam of light pierced the darkness of the theater. The small group of insurance company workers and firemen still in the auditorium looked upward and saw the ceiling of the house sagging in a horrific manner. Moments later, the mass gave way with a deafening groan, dropping thousands of pounds of flaming wreckage more than fifty feet to the floor of the house. Each of the men who had been in the theater safely fled before the collapse, but within the debris, more than two dozen firefighters lay injured, dying, and dead.

The men who fell were caught entirely unaware. Upon arriving at the scene, they assumed that the fire had started in the kitchen and that the massive joists that supported the auditorium's ceiling were undamaged. But as the men began to gather above the house, the joists had already nearly been burned through. Even without the weight of the men and the water they were pumping into the building, an expert later determined, the joists would have failed and doomed the theater.

More than a dozen water streams were aimed into the hellish pit just after the collapse, the work of rescue and recovery impossible until the flames were out. It was nearly an hour after the fire had been doused that the first body was pulled from the wreckage. The work was slow and grim, with massive timbers trapping the survivors. Many of the dead were so badly burned they could not easily be identified. One man was known only because of the number on the helmet that was still fastened to his head. The man's lower half was charred to such an extent that his feet were never recovered. "I saw death in a dozen horrible forms," said one man who was pulled from the mass.

As the missing were slowly accounted for, a faint voice emerged from far beneath a massive pile of debris. "I am John Crowley, and I am all right, but for God's sake, don't drown me here." It had been five hours since the collapse and at least three hours since any survivors had been recovered. Crowley was pinned beneath twelve feet of iron and wood, trapped near two more of the dead. Crowley yelled for a saw to cut off his legs so that he could be pulled to safety. His pleas were refused, but his urgency was understood. The thousands of gallons of water dumped into the pit were quickly gaining on him. Huge pumps were rushed to the scene to keep Crowley from drowning as crews worked to gingerly remove the several tons of material that trapped him. As the flames periodically leapt back to life, the crews retreated, sending streams of water down on their comrade, who was now breathing through a length of hose that had been lowered to him. At 12:14 p.m., more than seven hours after the collapse, a massive timber was removed and John Crowley was pulled to safety. He was taken to the hospital, but suffered only minor injuries. After his removal, several of the men who had worked to free him collapsed from exhaustion. It would still be another six hours before the final bodies were recovered.

In all, nine men perished and fifteen were injured in the Davidson disaster. In the weeks following the fire, an inquest determined that there was no blame to be laid with the construction of the roof or its support joists. Faulty wiring was believed to have been the cause of the fire. Insurance inspectors had twice relayed to the hotel's owners that the wiring was "dangerously defective" and badly in need of improvement. The most recent inspection occurred just weeks before the fire. No charges were ever filed in the matter.

THE GREAT HORROR

January 1883

"THE CALAMITY that has for years been predicted," the *Milwaukee Journal* wrote in a rushed extra edition, "has at last been visited upon Milwaukee." As these copies were hustled from the presses and into the city streets, the interior of Milwaukee's grandest hotel belched forth eruptions of flame and smoke that could be seen for miles. A few hours earlier, at about 3:30 a.m., an overnight lift operator was making his regular rounds at the Newhall House on Broadway and Michigan Street when he noticed gray ribbons of smoke leaking beneath the elevator doors on the hotel's sixth floor. He rushed to the ground level, where he notified the hotel's night clerk. The clerk ran outside and saw a horrible plume of smoke rushing from the building's Michigan Street entrance. As the clerk rang the number 15 firebox at Michigan and Broadway, the hotel engi-

neer—who, with the clerk and lift operator, constituted the hotel's entire overnight staff—yanked the nozzle of the building's
fire hose from its spooling and began to drag it down the hall
toward the blazing elevator shaft. But the aged rubber hose
cracked and split as it unspooled, rendering it useless. The hose
was the only real defense against fire that the hotel featured.
Despite the constant threat of fire—the building had often been
described as a "tinderbox" and had caught fire at least twenty
times since it opened in 1857—there were no fire alarms and
no in-house telephone system. The staff had long followed the
dictates of management that, in the case of smaller nighttime
fires, guests were not to be awoken. But as flames roared up
the wooden elevator shaft, the three-man staff of the Newhall
rushed through the building, violently kicking open doors and
screaming for guests to run for their lives.

By the time the first fire companies arrived on the scene,
flames shot from the windows along Michigan Street and the
heat of the upper floors had become so intense that some people
were burned to death in their beds without ever having touched
the flames. Members of the city's chemical engine rushed into
the building and gave a futile attempt to smother the flames at
the base of the elevator shaft. When it became clear this would
have no effect, they were ordered out and into the alley behind
the building, just off Michigan Street. Less than thirty minutes
after the sounding of the alarm, people were already beginning
to leap from the upper floors. Before firemen could procure the
department's jumping sheets, as many as a half-dozen broken
bodies lay mangled in the dim alleyway. Most of them were
young women who worked at the Newhall as servants. Their
sleeping quarters were located on the fifth floor, along the alley
side of the building. Without access to the hotel's few fire es-
capes and air so thick with heat and smoke, survival must have
seemed impossible, and many girls chose the instant relief of
the frozen bricks some one hundred feet down than the slow
and agonizing roast of the flames.

The Newhall House ablaze, as depicted by *Harper's* **Weekly**
WHi Image ID 54278

The fire department had only one ladder long enough to reach the upper floors. This tool was rendered useless after its first use, when the rescue of a heavyset man snapped it in two. As the flames broke through the roof of the building, escape from within was virtually impossible. By then, thousands of people had rushed into the snow-lined streets to see the great conflagration. As it became clear there was no way to rescue those on the fifth and sixth floors, the great crowds also witnessed a score of deaths that played out in gruesome desperation. From a single window ledge on the fifth floor, six people dangled by their fingers, dropping off one by one as their strength gave out. Those who tried to land on jumping sheets or in blankets held prone by citizens fared little better. Some leapt and missed their targets. Others made their mark, but fell through the thin fabric. At least one man's jump was interrupted by the maze of telegraph wires that spanned from the building, slicing him apart as he fell and drenching those beneath him in blood. One man managed to climb from his fifth-floor window to the decorative framing of the one below, then scaled down that window to perform the same act again. The crowds cheered him on as he made it from fourth to third and third to second. But atop the frame of the second-floor window, he lost his footing and fell, twisting during the short drop and landing headfirst on the pavement with a sickening crunch.

But the night did not pass without heroes. Brawny Herman Strauss, a former blacksmith whose Hook and Ladder Company Number 1 was the first on the scene that night, personally saved at least five women from the top floor of the building. Strauss was one of the men sent into the alleyway shortly after the first alarm. With no clear plan on how to reach the upper floors, Strauss and a man named George Wells—who worked in the nearby Goodyear Rubber factory—hauled a twenty-two-foot ladder to the roof of the neighboring Frackelton Building. From the roof, they swung the ladder across to the ledge of the Newhall's fifth floor. The span between the buildings was only about eighteen inches less than the length of the ladder, but, with Wells holding tightly at one end, Strauss made the trip across the bridge at least ten times, pulling five women from the doomed hotel and carrying them to safety atop the Frackelton. One woman, weighing in excess of two hundred pounds, fainted as Strauss carried her across and briefly dangled above the pavement as Strauss held tightly to her leg. On his last trip to the fifth floor, Strauss climbed inside the window and saw rumpled bodies laying all about the room, women who had fainted or had frozen in terror. He carried one more across the bridge before another company managed to raise another ladder to spot and rescue five more before the room was overtaken.

Within an hour of the first alarm, the entire interior of the hotel was ablaze. Shortly past 5:00 a.m., the sixth, fifth, and fourth floors gave way with an agonized groan. The collapse sent a plume of fire high into the frozen night air, and a stiff southerly wind pulled sparks and cinders into a terrific storm of flame that lit the evening sky as bright as day. For blocks in every direction, the hiss and roar of the furnace that the New-hall had become could be heard in sickening clarity. By now, the eighty-plus firefighters at the scene could only work to keep the neighboring buildings from becoming similarly engulfed. All that was left for the great fire to do was burn itself into submission. A reserve crew of men called up from Chicago was sent orders to turn around and head back. There was no one left to save. By 6:00 a.m., nothing was left of the Newhall but its flaming interior ruins and a brittle brick shell. This, too, soon gave way. As the sun rose on Milwaukee that day, the place that had opened as the "largest and finest hotel in the West" was a steaming, ice-coated pile of rubble. At the River Street morgue, bodies lay in heaps. And still dozens more were to be recovered from the ruins.

In the days after the fire, hundreds of volunteers went to work combing the wreckage for victims. In frigid weather, one tortured body after another was found in varying states of horror. "I've been on many a battlefield," a Civil War veteran aiding in the search told the *Milwaukee Sentinel*, "but I never saw such a horrible sight as the one I just viewed." Many of the remains recovered could not—and would never be—identified. The Newhall's register, the only list of exactly who was in the building that night, had been dropped by the clerk as he fled the building and was never recovered. A series of numbered boxes sat along the sidewalk, and one by one they were filled with the human parts the fire left behind. "I have seen bodies

torn and mangled," the vet continued. "But they retained some
semblance to human shape.... These are simply horrible."

Bodies were found with their arms and legs burned to nubs.
Many could only have their gender determined by examination of their internal organs. A small girl's shoe was found with
flesh burned to its leather. One woman was found to have been
literally baked to death in her bed. The body had not been exposed to the flames, but an outline of her female shape had been
roasted into the mattress on which she slept. She was placed in
box 21. Another body was found with its flesh burned away and
head reduced to ash. It was placed in box 16. Days later, the
stench of death still hung over the block. But neither that nor
the frigid temperatures could keep people from the scene. They
walked freely along the alleyway where so many of the young
women had died. They tried to enter the ruins of the building
to look around. "They hover above the ghastly remains," the
Sentinel wrote, "like a flock of vultures." When the blackened
and brittle remains of the west wall of the building was pushed
over, dozens rushed into the streets, but, in the words of the
Sentinel, "When it was found out that no one had been injured,
the multitude vanished as quickly as it came."

At a temporary morgue set up on Broadway, throngs of curious people pressed in to view the long line of numbered boxes.
The scene there was another awful one. The bodies lay out uncovered, and the mangled remains of the servant girls who had
jumped lay naked on tables. There were no sponges, no soap,
and no hot water. Eventually the crowds became so disruptive
that police allowed only those with a signed permit from the
mayor access to the building. The temporary morgue continued
to operate there until neighbors complained about the horrible
smell and the bodies were carted off to the River Street facility.

Six days after the fire, George Scheller, proprietor of the
hotel bar, was arrested on charges of arson. As sensational
claims about his business and personal dealings were reported in local and national papers, bodies continued to be pulled
from the rubble. With the official death count now topping fifty,

Scheller was visited by his lawyer at the central station. "I hope to God you are not guilty of this thing," were his first words to his client. The following day, Scheller was secreted out of the city due to threats of lynching. Scheller operated a saloon of ill-repute on Market Street, in the heart of the city's red-light district. He had connections to prostitution, was known to be in heavy debt, and allegedly had problems with both drinking and gambling. Rumors flew that his share in the hotel was insured for twice its value, and he had been seen moving six hundred dollars' worth of whiskey from the hotel's storerooms to his own saloon the night before the fire. Most troubling, though, were his whereabouts the night of the fire. Both he and his wife insisted that he had left the hotel at 1:30 a.m. and was in bed when the alarms rang out. But several witnesses placed him at an after-hours gambling den, stone drunk and playing cards until just before the fire broke out.

More than ten days after the fire, the final body—an unknown woman placed in box 48—was taken from the site. And still, a crowd remained to watch the work. These "odd freaks of the devouring flames," in the words of the *Sentinel*, drifted away soon after. On January 23, two mass funerals were held for forty-three victims of the fire—of the estimated 74 total— who could not be identified. Those thought to be domestics were given a Catholic service, and those thought to be guests were buried as Protestants. The caskets and burial services were provided free of charge. Herman Strauss was lauded as a hero for his role in rescuing the trapped girls of the fifth floor. He was mostly uncomfortable with the attention. "I only did my duty," he said just after the fire, "[and] acted as the department taught us." In a special ceremony to present him with a gold watch and chain from the Chamber of Commerce, he was invited to give a speech to the hundreds of assembled persons. Strauss fumbled for a few moments before acknowledging his mother and leaving the podium.

In April, George Scheller went on trial. In the months since the fire, the public had rallied heavily to Scheller's side. No evidence was ever produced connecting him with the lighting of the fire. Beyond the rumors of his personal trouble, there remained only the disparity over his whereabouts on the night in question. He eventually admitted to lying to protect the other men who had been with him at the illegal card game that night. After a weeklong trial, the jury took two hours to find him not guilty. A great cheer went up in the courtroom when the verdict was read, and hundreds of grinning supporters followed Scheller through the streets as he left the courthouse a free man.

DEATH ON THE QUEEN
June 1917

THE SS *Christopher Columbus* was filled to less than one-tenth of its five-thousand-person capacity as it was being towed stern-first down the Milwaukee River. The 360-foot excursion vessel was launched in 1892, built for the Columbian Exposition at Chicago. The only whaleback-style passenger boat ever built, it was outfitted with electric lighting, a grand promenade deck, several fountains, an aquarium, and state rooms detailed in marble, velvet, and etched glass. Billed as the "Queen of the Lakes," the *Columbus* ferried as many as two million passengers on Lake Michigan tours during the six months of the exposition.

After the close of the exposition, the *Columbus* began regular passenger service on the lakes. By 1906, the boat was making daily runs from Chicago to Milwaukee, docking in the Cream City at the Goodrich Transport terminal on the Milwaukee River, just south of the Michigan Street Bridge. In order to make its way off of the dock and out to the lake, the massive boat ran backward down the narrow river. When the vessel reached the point where the Milwaukee River met the Menomonee and bent to the east, the twin tugs assisting it would pull the stern of the boat up the Menomonee as far as the Milwaukee Road railroad bridge, allowing it to swing its bow roughly forty-five degrees, aiming it down the united riverways and out toward the lake. In eleven years of regular service between the two cities, the *Columbus* and its crew had executed this maneuver thousands of times without incident.

Heavy rains had pounded Milwaukee in the days before the tugs *Welcome* and *Knight Templar* aided the *Columbus* downriver as the ship departed on its 4:30 p.m. trip to Chicago. The passenger load of about four hundred was light for a Saturday. Alumni of the University of Chicago made up about half of the group, having just completed their annual outing to the north. Quartermaster James Brody was at the wheel that afternoon, overseen by Captain James Moody, who was in his thirteenth year in command of the *Columbus*. Moody had noticed the high waters of the river upon departure, but he noted no trouble until the *Columbus*'s stern hit the mouth of the Menomonee. The rains had drenched the valley that formed the river's watershed and the waters meeting the Milwaukee River were flowing much harder than usual.

The *Columbus* after its Milwaukee River wreck
WHi Image ID 33123

Immediately, Moody knew something was amiss. The swing of the boat's bow was arching far too close to the eastern bank of the river. He ordered the ship's engines reversed to slow the turn and give the tugs more time to pull against the heavy flow of the Menomonee. But the river's speed could not be overcome. Moody knew at that moment, he later testified, that "a serious accident could not be avoided." The boat was about fifty feet from the riverbank. Moody grabbed a megaphone and yelled to a group of passengers standing on the deck at the still-moving bow of the boat. He screamed for them to clear out of the area, but they either did not hear or ignored his warning. He shouted again but to no effect. "Had they obeyed," he later said, "no one would have been hurt."

The unique design of the *Columbus* gave it a long bow that arched gently from the water. As the imperiled boat swung, its long nose missed the low-lying bulkhead along the river, but it could not avoid one of the wooden support legs of a one-hundred-foot-tall water tower that sat behind the Yahr and Lang Drug building on East Water Street. The leg snapped clean off about twenty feet from the ground and the weight of the tank's contents began to tip it slowly toward the river. Had the *Columbus* been able to make it just two feet farther up the Menomonee, it would have missed the tower completely.

With the dreadful snapping of heavy timbers and the sharp ricochet of its support cables being pulled from the brick buildings behind it, the tower fell awkwardly over the five decks of the *Columbus*. The tank fell clear of the boat's starboard side, but the support structure crushed the port side of the vessel like an eggshell, ripping a twelve-foot gash in the roof of the dining room. The wheelhouse was smashed, and dozens of passengers were sent flying in all directions. Many ended up in the river, while a few unfortunates were torn apart by the collapse, their blood streaking the deck of the boat and running into the water.

"The breaking of the timber, the yells of the boathands, and the screams of the women will stick to me as long as I live," a survivor told the *Milwaukee Journal*. "The whole boat rocked and careened as if it was going over.... One woman had her head mashed into a jelly. Another had her legs cut completely off. And I saw them gathering up the heart and organs of some other person. I tried to get through and help, but they wouldn't let me."

After the crash, the tugs pulled the wounded boat to the opposite side of the river, where it was quickly tied up. As doctors rushed to the scene, and the crew lined up the dead and wounded in the dining room, thousands gathered along the river to glimpse the awful scene. By that evening, officials could still not say how many had been killed. Many had simply fled the boat after it had docked, making an accurate accounting of the passenger list impossible. Through the night, crews dragged the river for bodies as police tried to identify those who had been recovered. One man, Thomas Creel, was identified by letters found in his breast pocket. One woman was known only by a card she carried with the word *Alta* written on it. Another man had nothing on his person but a watch fob and sixteen cents.

In the days that followed the wreck, the death toll settled at sixteen—all eventually identified—with dozens more injured. An inquest into the incident the following week absolved Captain Moody and his crew, as well as the tugboat crews, of any wrongdoing. This was, the inquest determined, a disaster not of man's making, but the tragic result of something beyond mortal control.

THE *ALLEGHANY*
September 1850

A S THE steamer *Alleghany* limped through Milwaukee Harbor, it carried with it the foul air of death. The 260-

passenger vessel, arriving from Buffalo, was thick with typhoid fever. During the weeks-long Great Lakes journey, the boat spanned Lakes Erie and Huron, passing through the Straits of Mackinac and riding the rolling waters of Lake Michigan south toward Milwaukee. Somewhere along the way, the deadly virus spread among the passengers. The first days of a typhoid fever infection brought about high fever, headaches, coughs, and a thin stream of blood from the nose. After a week, the victim was too weak to stand, overcome with fever and mild delirium. Red spots appeared on the skin, and intense and painful diarrhea occurred. After two weeks, the grim comfort of death was not far. Severe dehydration and "muttering delirium" overtook the infected, causing victims to constantly tug at their clothes or imaginary objects. The red spots turned to bloody abscesses. Intestinal bleeding and perforations caused intense pain. By the time the fetid boat reached the city, twenty-five passengers had already died. During the vessel's first hours in port, another eight succumbed, with more than forty feebly clinging to life.

Ever cautious of the potential havoc to be wrought by infectious disease, the city's board of health ordered the passengers to disembark on the marshy little slip of lakefront land that rested between the Milwaukee River and Lake Michigan. An abandoned tumbledown shack sat on the land, used by government workers some years earlier during the construction of the harbor. The city tasked the local Sisters of Charity chapter with caring for the passengers, who would be quarantined at the site, now termed the city "pest house," for three weeks. Just 60 of the 260 souls aboard the *Alleghany* would live long enough to be allowed in the city proper.

The tragedy of the *Alleghany* had been nearly forgotten by 1856, when the Jones Shipbuilding Company was operating on what was by then known as Jones Island, near the location of the old pest house. In June of that year, the company launched the largest boat, and the first propeller-driven vessel, yet built in Milwaukee. Just hours after being launched, however, the boat ran aground in foul weather, driving its hull deep into the soil of the island. As crews worked with a steam dredge to free the vessel, they uncovered a horrific sight: ghastly white bones—femurs, rib cages, and skulls—hidden beneath mere inches of soil. It was the vast burial grounds from the typhoid boat of 1850, the ignoble resting place of nearly two hundred men, women, and children who had known America only long enough to die there.

In a coincidental twist, this boat had also been christened *Alleghany.* Jones's *Alleghany* remained lodged in the marshy earth of the island for another ten months before a house-moving firm was finally able to free it. Shortly after the vessel's relaunch, it was involved in a collision and sank.

"AN OCEAN GRAVEYARD"
October 1929

THE *MILWAUKEE JOURNAL* called the wicked northerly gale that pounded Lake Michigan that day "the greatest freshwater blow in sixteen years." The winds topped fifty miles per hour, lashing across miles of open lake, driving waves up to twenty feet, and churning Milwaukee Bay into a frigid and terrible froth. As snow and hail pelted the city, crews quickly loaded the train ferry SS *Milwaukee* at its dock at the north end of the Kinnickinnic River. The *Milwaukee*, captained by Robert "Bad Weather Bob" McKay, had just come through the storm, arriving earlier in the day from Grand Haven, Michigan. After being loaded in Milwaukee, it was to head back to Grand Haven, but the weather had fouled considerably since the vessel's stormy arrival. At the dockworker's union headquarters on Milwaukee's south side, two crew members of the ferry, due to make the return trip, did not even bother to make their way to the dock. There was no chance, they thought, that Captain McKay would go out in such dangerous conditions.

**This novelty postcard doctored a photo of the SS *Milwaukee*
having its stern tipped out of the water for routine maintenance to give the impression the great boat was sinking.**
Great Lakes Marine Collection of the Milwaukee Public Library / Wisconsin
Marine Historical Society

But just past 3:00 p.m., to the amazement of its crew, the *Milwaukee*'s departure whistle sounded and the lumbering vessel
slowly pushed away from its dock. Aboard were fifty-two crew
members and more than one hundred thousand dollars' worth
of cargo. The *Milwaukee* was designed to carry fully loaded
train cars in its hold, a cheaper and faster alternative to sending railcars around the lake. As it got underway on that stormy
afternoon, the ferry was loaded with twenty-seven cars packed
with everything from automobiles to bathtubs to cheese. As the
Milwaukee headed through the outer harbor and past the confines of the breakwater walls, a group of men watched from
the windows of the ten-story Elks Club building on Wisconsin
Avenue. They saw the great ship tossed violently, nearly disap-
pearing when it fell into the trough of the huge waves the storm
had produced. One of the men asked another what chances he
felt the boat had of surviving. "Fifty-fifty," he replied.

The man's assessment was optimistic. Three miles off shore, the *Milwaukee* passed a United States Coast Guard lightship, which later reported the boat to be rolling badly. The ship lost sight with the *Milwaukee* at 3:45 p.m. It was the last vessel to report contact with the ferry. About seven miles off shore, as the boat pitched steeply in the roaring seas, a chain used to hold a set of railcars in place in the cargo hold snapped, allowing the load to slide violently across the hold. The cars smashed into the boat's storm gate, punching a fatal gash through the hull. As the hull rapidly took water, Captain McKay made a futile attempt to make it back to shore, but the wounded boat could not overcome the storm. The *Milwaukee* met the lake bottom about three miles off of Fox Point.

The next morning, all corners of Lake Michigan were assessing the brutal storm's toll. Millions of dollars in damage were reported from across the region. Five ships were immediately known to be lost, with several more badly damaged or grounded. At least three people had drowned in the treacherous seas. In Milwaukee, eight hundred feet of the breakwater wall had been washed away. The clubhouse of the South Shore Yacht Club was leveled. Ships long past due in the city finally limped into port, hours off their schedules and with crew and passengers grateful to have survived.

The morning papers breathlessly reported on the damage wrought but hardly mentioned the *Milwaukee*. The commander of the Grand Truck Railroad fleet, owners of the ferry, proclaimed his utter faith in Captain McKay, citing his fifty years' experience on the lake. "Because he is in charge of the *Milwaukee*, I am not generally worried," the man said. "Captain McKay is familiar with every nook and cove on Lake Michigan and he very likely has found one in which to ride out the storm."

But worries grew as the hours ticked by. The SS *Grand Rapids*, another Grand Truck ferry, had by the next day arrived safely in Michigan, having left four hours after the *Milwaukee* and reporting no sight of the vessel. Later that day, the SS *Cetus*, a steel freighter bound for Milwaukee from Chicago, came upon gruesome wreckage just off Kenosha. One, then another and another appeared around the boat, dead men strapped into SS *Milwaukee* life vests. "All about us they were hovering," the *Cetus*'s captain reported, "like tombstones in an ocean graveyard."

Three bodies were pulled from the water near Kenosha. Another two were found near Chicago. Soon, great chunks of the doomed vessel were reported floating near various ports. On Saturday, a lifeboat was found off Holland, Michigan. It carried four frigid bodies, tied into the same lifejackets found on the others. An examination of the bodies determined they had perished sometime on Friday, survivors of the wreck who died of exposure in the days that followed. Of the fifty-two men lost with the ship, only these nine were ever recovered.

The day after the discovery of the four bodies, another lifeboat was found near South Haven, Michigan. A waterproof case was the boat's only occupant. Inside was a scrawled note: "The ship is making water fast," it read in part. "We have turned around and headed for Milwaukee.... Seas are tremendous. Things look bad. Crew roll is about the same as the last payday."

LAUNCH OF THE *WILLIAM H. WOLF*
August 1887

A CROWD of three thousand had turned out to see the launch of the *William H. Wolf*, the largest boat yet built on the Great Lakes. The 308-foot steamer had been built at the renowned Wolf and Davidson Shipyards, located on the western shore of Milwaukee's inner harbor, just across from the Jones Island fishing village. It was named in honor of the firm's cofounder and was being launched on his fifty-ninth birthday.

The huge throngs of people—the largest crowd ever to witness a boat launch in city history—lined the streets and shorelines. They stood perched on log pilings and roofs and huddled on fishing boats and in canoes. Hundreds lined the decks of the steamer *Gordon*, which had docked nearby for the ceremony. And about five hundred more had a prime view of the launch, standing atop a wooden track along the Wolf and Davidson coal houses. The track was about twenty feet wide and stood twenty feet off the ground.

At 3:40, the great boat slid down a set of wooden skids and dropped into the harbor. A mighty cheer went up from the crowd, a band tooted out happy songs, and steam whistles blew all across the harbor. But as the *Wolf* uprighted itself in the harbor, a huge swell of water displaced by its mass unexpectedly leapt onto the land. The wave crashed over some ten feet of dock and rushed forward, wiping out the support beams of a section of coal track on which as many as seventy-five people stood. The platform fell with a terrifying crash, and dozens of onlookers were washed into the harbor. Tormented screams were heard in every direction as people thrashed about helplessly in the agitated waters. The watching boats rushed to the scene to pull the injured from the water. More than three dozen were hurt in the collapse. One man drowned in the frothy harbor during the aftermath of the collapse while another, seventeen-year-old Eddie Zerbell, was found dead of a broken neck underneath the wreckage of the platform. In the panic and confusion that followed the launch, it was impossible to determine if all those who had been standing on the platform were accounted for. Police spent two hours that evening dragging the river for more bodies.

William H. Wolf blamed the platform's collapse on the crowd's rush forward at the moment of the launch. He claimed to have seen the supports give way before the wave touched the shore. No one else made similar claims. In the days after the accident, an estimated ten thousand people visited the scene of the collapse, filing past in a near constant stream during all daylight hours. "It's an ill wind that blows nobody good," a

peanut vendor remarked to the *Milwaukee Sentinel*. The man
had set up his cart near the spot and reported to the paper that
he had been doing very good business there.

IN THE CRIB
April 1893

A TERRIBLE spring storm began to lash the Milwaukee harbor
in the early-morning hours of April 19. The temperatures
lingered just above freezing as a wicked easterly gale churned
Lake Michigan to a hellish froth. Some three thousand feet off
the North Point shoreline, fifteen workmen huddled inside a
wooden shack that stood atop the yet-unfinished city intake
crib. The house was the temporary living quarters for the men
building the crib—a one-hundred-foot-wide octagon that shel-
tered a twenty-foot-wide circular iron shaft, which was to span
from ten feet above the water line to eighty feet beneath. The
shaft was cleared of lake water as it was sunk and would ultimately link the North Point pumping station with intake pipes
that extended another five thousand feet into the lake, drawing
in water to be pumped into city reservoirs for public use.

As the sun trembled upward through the angry April sky,
the men went about their regular routine, working to sink the
massive rounded steel shaft pieces yet deeper into the lake bed.
But just after darkness fell, the still-furious waves knocked a
portion of the wooden shack from its perch. Soon after, the engine and boiler—which had been fasted to the top of the crib
with eighteen-inch steel bolts—were similarly brushed away.
The tremendous seas made escape back to land impossible, so
the men climbed into the crib and spent the night hidden in
the air-locked shaft. As the storm continued to pound Milwaukee, the families of the crew members stared into the blackened
lake with alarm. The red lantern that had always shone from
the house atop the crib could not be seen. Wives of the men

anxiously sought out the project's engineers. "They are down below," the engineers assured the women. "Wait until morning."

Inside the shaft, the air pressure was twice that of normal conditions. The evening was dry but restless for the men. Against the locked gate above them, they could hear lake water collecting in the exposed end of the crib. By morning, the storm had yet to break and the thick air of the shaft was beginning to take a toll. The men weakened as their blood thinned and breathing became labored. Escape to open air was possible, but there was no way to tell how much water had collected in the top of the crib overnight. At 7:00 a.m., one of the men lit a match to check his pocket watch. The tiny flame revealed that two of his fellow workers had already suffocated. "We have got to go," someone muttered in the dark. It was decided unanimously to open the hatch and risk the storm.

"I knew there was water in the shaft above us," thirty-three-year-old crib worker James Miller later said. "But I thought that there was not much of it." Miller was chosen by the men to be the one to open the hatch above them. Later described by the *Milwaukee Journal* as "a perfect giant...nothing but brawn and muscle," Miller turned the heavy locks of the hatch shortly after 8:00 a.m. When he broke the seal on the hatch, a deathly torrent of water rushed past him. Unknown to the men, the top section of the shaft had nearly filled completely and held about ten feet of water by the time the decision to flee had been made. After prying open the man-sized hatch, nearly six thousand gallons of water poured over the men. Miller and five others made it out. Six could not and were drowned within minutes.

As the men struggled to the top of the crib, a crowd gathered on the beach, focusing their distant gaze on the structure, hoping for any signs of life. As daylight broke that morning, the wreckage of the ruined shack was found strewn about Bradford Beach. It had been clear for hours that a rescue mission to the crib was needed, but no competent seaman had yet volunteered to tempt the still-tremendous seas. At 9:30 a.m., a small white flag was seen fluttering above the crib, and six gaunt figures appeared at its peak. A cheer went up from the crowd, but the mood quickly dulled when they realized that several miles of terrible seas still had to be covered if there was to be any hope of saving the men. At 10:00 a.m., a tugboat started out the Jones Island life-saving station, but was forced to turn back after nearly capsizing. Meanwhile, the six men atop the crib clung desperately to the support cables that crisscrossed the structure as the lake churned all around them. Over the next hour, four of the men lost their grip and slipped away, pulled in by the lake and ferried from this world.

Finally, at 11:00 a.m., the storm began to break. By 11:20, the tug *Welcome* started off for the crib from the life-saving station at Jones Island with a crew of four. Helmed by Captain Ingar Olsen, the tug was approaching the site just as John McBride, a thirty-five-year-old engineer from Chicago, slipped from the cable and sank into the water. "Poor fellow," Miller said later. "If he had only held out ten minutes longer he would [have survived]." The waters about the crib were still rolling wildly and the *Welcome* circled it three times trying to find an opening to dock. Unable to find one, the tug dropped its little lifeboat about two hundred feet off. Crewmen rowed the boat near the crib and tossed a life rope into the opening. When no one took the line after several tries, it appeared that the entire roster of workmen had perished. Unwilling to leave without visual confirmation of the dead, Captain Olsen leapt from the little lifeboat onto the side of the crib. Inside, he saw a horrific tangle of lifeless bodies floating among the scraps of the crib's wrecked superstructure. And he found big James Miller clinging to life. Pulling Miller onto his back, he climbed back to the boat, paddled to the tug, and brought the lone survivor of the Milwaukee crib disaster back to the mainland.

The next morning, the steamer *Burroughs* took a recovery crew to the crib. Ten bodies were found inside with another four later recovered at the shore. The *Milwaukee Journal* described the scene as a "confused mass of arms and legs." In the icy water, the limbs of the victims had contorted themselves into horrible shapes. As the bodies were fished from the shaft with a grappling pole, the steamer's crew forced them flat so they could be laid out on the deck. A crib worker named Frank Brown, who had been on just his second day on the job, was found with his hands rigidly clamped together and knees bowed, as if in the position of prayer.

After emptying the shaft of its terrible contents, a crewman raised two arms high and extended ten fingers, the signal to the masses still watching from the beach that ten bodies had been found. The boat lowered its flag to half-mast as it made the sad trip back to land. The crowds from the beach joined with others and marched by foot along the banks of the Milwaukee River. As the boat made its slow procession to the docks at East Water Street, hundreds stared in grim silence at the ten lifeless shapes on its decks. "Many a strong-hearted person," the *Journal* wrote, "turned away sick and faint at the ghastly sight."

Captain Olsen was awarded the US Coast Guard Lifesaving Medal for his actions in saving James Miller. An inquest into the disaster found no fault to be assigned for deaths. They were, merely, the unfortunates of an act of God.

VICE

A CITY IS built on desires: the mad lusts to rule and conquer, the heartfelt needs of community and companionship, the fevered drives for freedom and democracy. These were the desires that wrested Milwaukee from its native residents, flooded its spaces with a patchwork of new peoples and cultures, and built its mighty engines of business and industry. And in Milwaukee, with its raw and hard-worked citizenry just as eager to spend a buck as to earn it, an underground economy of desire grew both in plain sight and in the darkened corners of the city.

The desires displayed in these tales of vice are recognizable and relatable as achingly honest outgrowths of the human condition. Yet these indulgences, the thrills of flesh, chance, and intoxication, have often been seen as something like a trip too near to the sun. To partake in them openly and in wanton disregard for the ostensible standards of the community was to actively court censure. Moreover, behind each ripe pleasure were cases of sorrow and heartbreak that reformers quickly seized upon as reasons for action. Then, as now, the moral panics displayed in these tales of vice appear as reflexive attempts to pull the brakes on a place moving too fast for its own good.

Heels or sports, victims or crooks, sinners or survivors— whether they needed salvation or not, time has laid them all upon an equal plane. In the spirit of that old axiom that urges one to pray for the living and not the dead, these dark-cornered troubles of old Milwaukee are now ours. And while we are occasionally shocked by the goings-on in these dark places today, the city is never shocked. It has seen it all before.

GAMES OF CHANCE
May 1895

A GROUP of Milwaukee's Methodist ministers assailed both
Mayor John Koch and Chief of Police John Janssen for
what they saw as a sinful laxity in enforcing the city laws that
forbade the operation of gambling parlors. While none directly accused either man of operating in cahoots with gambling
forces, they accused both of allowing the city police department
to be infiltrated by gaming influences. Certain beat officers,
Reverend George Ide claimed, were working as intermediaries
for gambling dens, directing strangers in search of "the tiger"
to saloons and halls that would later reward the officers with
kickbacks. More still were deeply concerned by Chief Janssen's
unwillingness to execute raids on known gaming spots. Reverend Henry Coleman said this attitude was attracting rogues
to Milwaukee and that other cities had developed a habit of
dumping their criminals—he considered all gamblers, thieves,
and grain speculators to be criminals of an unvaried lot—at its
doorstep. "We have begun this warfare to win," Reverend E. L.
Eaton told the mayor and chief. "And from this [day] on, it shall
be a fight to the finish."

But the reverends came to Koch and Janssen with more
than just complaints. They also brought firsthand knowledge
of the city's gaming scene. On three different evenings during
early 1895, the three trusted men of the church headed out into
the Badlands, the pocket of west-of-the-river Milwaukee—running roughly from the river to Sixth Street and from Wisconsin
Avenue to State Street—where gambling, prostitution, and dive
saloons operated openly and without fear of the law. Most of the
spots they found offered faro, craps, roulette, and poker. The
smallest was the backroom of Schofer's Saloon on Second Street
between Grand Avenue and Wells Street. Despite the tight confines, the men found more than forty gamblers crowded into the

place, coaxed to the tables by a barker who called out, "Come along, boys! Everybody invited to throw." At 417 East Water Street, in a den hidden in the upper floors of a building that housed a saloon, they found nearly seventy-five men crowded around various tables, all urged by a leather-lunged dealer to "try their luck."

Four men stage a scene that was a regular sight in Milwaukee's Badlands.
WHi Image ID 34529

Above Weber's Saloon, just across the street at 410 East Water, the action was kept behind a door at the top of a long staircase. Five tables were found in the room, each manned by a keeper who was "very pressing" in his solicitations. A few blocks away, at 333 Broadway, the men came upon "the toniest den in town." The parlor was kept above the Marble Hall saloon, hidden behind a maple door with a "small diamond hole." Inside, a well-dressed and divinely polite individual greeted the men and directed them to the dual gaming rooms. On the other end of the spectrum, and the other side of the river, was 107 Wells Street. The group considered this place to be "primarily for colored men." Of the thirty-four men found there, they reported that just "a few" were white and referred to the rest as "colored" or "Chinamen."

The ministers insisted that these experiences represented only the tip of Milwaukee's gambling den iceberg. They urged that the city's laws be directed to "protect the individual who is weak against the criminal rapacity of the strong." The gambling establishment of the city was to blame for "breaking up homes, crushing hearts, impoverishing the innocent, [and] producing embezzlement, robbery, murder, and suicide," a statement from the reverends claimed. "And those who are sworn to execute the law against these criminals seem to have no thought for an instant of doing so."

The Milwaukee Rescue Mission at the corner of Wells and Second Street. This house of charity was located within sight of dozens of gambling dens, dive saloons, and brothels.
Historic Photo Collection / Milwaukee Public Library

During their lambasting by the parsons, the mayor and chief stuck to their position that to act too aggressively against these houses would simply chase them from one dim part of the city to another. They said that when the police received a complaint of a man so badly "fleeced" by the dens that he could no longer afford to support his family, they would "generally" act in an attempt to get the establishment to repay the funds lost. After considering the case presented by the Methodists, Mayor Koch remained unmoved, telling the *Milwaukee Journal* that he had no intention of changing his policy on the matter. "Milwaukee is freer of the social evils of any other city of its size in the nation, as far as I know," he said. "It seems to me there is no occasion for the clergymen making all this fuss."

POLICY

September 1883

A STAGE show closed at the Academy of Music theater on Broadway after a short and unprofitable run. The *Milwaukee Sentinel* noted both the lethargic performance of its New Orleans Minstrel acting troupe and the sparse population of the academy's several thousand seats, writing that few cared to "witness the funeral performances of these alleged comedians."

But it was not acting, songs, or comedy that the show's manager, Frank Dalzell, had expected to draw people into the house. Instead, it was the chance to openly participate in one of the city's most popular illicit activities—the underground lottery known as policy. One of the show's skits was an ostensible exposé of the policy game, during which a series of numbers was randomly selected. If an audience member could guess what these numbers would be, Dalzell vowed to present the person with a thousand dollars in cash.

The show was a last-ditch attempt by Dalzell to salvage the legality of policy in the state, where calls were growing thick for stricter laws against the practice. Dalzell was a policy pioneer in Wisconsin, founding the first such operation in the state in Milwaukee in 1870. The street version of the game was similar to that of the stage show. Policy players picked numbers from between 1 and 78. A player could either play a single number, a "saddle" of two numbers, or a "gig" of three. The more numbers in the sequence, the more the player could win if his or her series matched the winning numbers.

The winning numbers were drawn twice daily in the little town of Covington, Kentucky, where the syndicate to which Dalzell belonged was headquartered. After being drawn in Covington, the numbers were wired to all affiliated cities via a ciphered telegram. At noon and 6:00 p.m., the numbers hit Milwaukee. Here, they would be relayed to Dalzell's several dozen "sub-agents"—neighborhood bookies who took bets for the central office and paid out cash to the winners. These men operated out of barbershops or bars, with at least one occupying nearly every corner of the city. Spots like Planthaber's Saloon at 109 West Water Street or the S. J. Hunt Rookery on Second Street had their regular policy agents, taking bets from a steady stream of customers all day long and memorizing hundreds of number combinations. As policy operations were given to police harassment, Dalzell ordered his agents to keep an absolute minimum of physical evidence of their trade.

"The negroes are inveterate policy players," wrote the *Sentinel*, "but in this city the game found its warmest and most liberal patrons among the stolid slow-going German workingmen and women." Those who played regularly devoted various kinds of pseudoscience to the selection of their numbers. Many devoted players kept charts of the selected numbers, studying their patterns and hidden trends. Many players felt that their dreams held the secrets to cracking the policy code. Publishers printed "dream books," which alleged to be able to translate the images of dreams into lucky number sequences. And still others played the same sequence endlessly, trusting that their patience would eventually pay off.

Shortly after the show at the Academy of Music closed, the state passed legislation that officially placed Dalzell on the wrong side of the law. But Dalzell had already built himself an empire, the most visible manifestation of which was his palatial home at Twenty-first Street and Grand Avenue. Despite his detractors, Dalzell never wavered in his insistence that his trade was legit. "My business...is carried on in deference to a demand," he was quoted as saying. "[It is] more honorable than the board of trade."

LONELY CORNERS
April 1894

E LECTION FEVER had overtaken Milwaukee when the *Milwaukee Sentinel* sent a man into the bowels of the Badlands to report on what was both one of the most prominent and one of the most secretive issues of the campaign—the dive bar. While the area's brothels operated with little interference from police, its seedy, low-end, hardscrabble saloons had for several years been raising the ire of reformers. These were places where beer and whiskey ran all night long as gaudily attired musicians ground out jaunty and vulgar tunes and prostitutes, too unreliable or surly to find residence in a proper brothel, plied their trade among the rough characters of Milwaukee's dark hours. There was also the alarming new development of the so-called stall saloon. Establishments with by-the-hour rooms on the upper floors had long been a regular feature of the area. But the stall saloon dropped such pretense and offered couples a quick kind of privacy in cheaply built, partitioned "stalls" located in back hallways or along the side walls of the bar.

Reformers had tried for years to eliminate the dive via licensing restrictions but with little success. A recent drive to close thirty-two "nests of infamy" resulted in the common council renewing the licenses of nearly all of them. The *Sentinel* cited the "powerful friends" of the dive keeper as a primary reason. Among those who opposed the dive was Mayor John

Koch, winner of a special election in July 1893. Among those who felt the dive should be left alone was Alderman Herman Fehr. He had voted regularly to approve the license applications of places considered among the worst in the city. As the *Sentinel* man headed into the darkness of Milwaukee's Badlands that mild April night, Koch and Fehr were just days away from squaring off in the spring election for mayor. The Badlands were undoubtedly Fehr country, but with Mayor Koch and his appointees still helming the city government, times in the district were very tight.

The reporter's first stop was at the River Street hall of H. L. Dietrichs. Previously known as the "lowest and toughest dive in the city" and often populated by the "worst class of prostitutes and loafers," it was one of the few denied a license renewal. The man found only soda water being served at the bar but still found it populated with various rough characters and working women. Along a long hallway behind the bar there had once been a series of stalls, but the reporter noticed that they had been removed, a nod to the tentative political climate of the city. The *Sentinel* man noticed "the soft drinks were not very much sought after" and that the female occupants of the place, with their "gauzy costumes and painted faces," hardly carried the same enthusiasm as they had the year before.

From the dim situation at Dietrichs's, the reporter visited a pair of troublesome stall saloons run by a local rounder named John Sheldon. He stopped first at Sheldon's Wells Street spot, located near an alleyway so thick with dead-end rumholes it was occasionally referred to as the "Bucket of Blood." The street entrance for this place led to a small, unfurnished room with a tiny bar and lunch counter. Eventually, the bartender asked the man if he would like to sit down. He replied that he would. The bartender pushed aside an icebox kept behind the bar to reveal a small doorway. The door led down a hallway to a larger room, where the action was concealed. The reporter took a seat and through another entrance "two robust female forms appeared."

They carried the same worn weariness as did the women of his previous stop. "They are fat," the man wrote, "and once might have been fair." The women sat with the reporter and took up his offer for drinks—hard liquor ordered by pressing a button connected to a bell at the outer bar. The bartender seemed to "know their drinks by intuition," the man observed. The women said they had arrived in the city from Omaha and, thus far, did not like Milwaukee.

He headed next to Sheldon's Third Street saloon, a far less covert place in which he found no females at all. A few of the men loafing around wore Fehr badges on their jackets. The bartender said that business had been slow ever since Holy Week, when police pulled five girls—presumably underage—from the place.

Al Schissler's place, at 236 Fourth Street, was visited next. Police had taken young girls from here as well and, like many trouble spots in the Badlands, it had been under police surveillance for some time. Schissler's featured a dozen stalls on the first and second floors, each connected to the main bar by a buzzer that was used to call for drinks. A few stalls were occupied during the reporter's visit, the drunken voices and tough language of their occupants plainly heard over the wooden partitions that shielded them from public viewing. A portrait of Herman Fehr hung behind the bar, just above the drink buzzer.

A few more stops confirmed the sad and strained times of the Badlands' dives. The bartender at Mulcahey's saloon at 174 Fifth Street said business had been slow in the lead-up to the election. His stock of politically connected regulars was afraid to be seen there. The Columbia, at 134 Third Street, was lively when the reporter stopped in, but the mood quickly soured when a pair of plainclothes police officers showed up in search of two underage girls known to frequent the place. The girls managed to slip out a back door before being spotted.

Days later, Koch whipped Fehr at the polls by a plurality of more than five thousand votes. The sour mood in the Badlands was expected to lift after the vote, as politicians freed from the fear of pre-election scandal would return to their favorite dives and re-elected officials would loosen the squeeze they had been placing on the area.

THE QUEEN OF NIGHTS
July 1884

"ROSINA IS a small woman—a frail being of the inferior sex—but she is bigger than the city of Milwaukee." Thus editorialized the *Milwaukee Sentinel* in the midst of one of Rosina Georg's frequent tussles with city authorities. "She snaps her fingers in the face of the reformatory mayor who never succeeds at reforming anything; she holds the entire Common Council in contempt—and she makes a sidewalk of the city attorney, walking all over him as regular as she meets him."

Rosina Georg, a slight, raven-haired woman of about forty years, inherited a dance hall and saloon at Eighth Street and Galena in 1878 after the death of her husband, William. Under her management, the place—known as Johannesburg—became one of the most notorious in the city. It was known as a spot that openly served alcohol to minors and allowed for the drunken social mixing of whites and blacks. Johannesburg also hosted raucous Sunday night dances, events that wantonly disregarded both the accepted custom and official law of the city. In October 1882, after a litany of complaints against the hall, the common council's licensing committee denied Rosina a saloon permit.

And so began open warfare between Rosina and the city. During this time, she was arrested no fewer than ten times for operating a saloon without a license, nearly every time managing to skirt conviction with the careful lawyering of her personal attorney, R. N. Austin. After being hustled into court for selling a slug of whiskey to an undercover police officer in

August 1883, Austin asked the court for an affidavit verifying that the saloon licensing ordinance had been published into the public record. When the court could produce no such documentation, he argued on technical grounds for the complete revocation of the ordinance. Indeed, the loophole he found—and the city's failure to adhere to it—voided the city's saloon licensing regulations under which Rosina had been arrested. In addition to tossing the permit law, Judge James Mallory stated that, in his opinion, Austin's discovery essentially voided all legislation passed by the common council for the past six years. Once again, Rosina walked from the courthouse a free woman, city authorities scrambling in her wake to pass legislation to restore the rule of law to Milwaukee.

"Rosina is not in the habit of trying to establish her innocence of any alleged infractions of the law," the *Sentinel* wrote. "She simply demonstrates the unconstitutionality of the law. She is becoming a howling terror to the legislative body." After the city's saloon ordinance was rewritten to meet with the requirements of the law, Rosina attempted to run her saloon as a stock company. Instead of drinks, she sold her patrons "shares" in a keg of beer, of which, the *Sentinel* wrote, "the festive lady acts as manager."

Through it all, Rosina never stopped trying to secure her license. She was a regular visitor to Mayor Emil Wallber's office, speaking with him in her native German and always carrying the $37.50 permit fee in her purse. "If they don't give me a license, I will run without one," she told a reporter. "I prefer to stop this trouble, though." In early July 1884, almost two years after her license was initially revoked, Rosina announced that Johannesburg was now a private club. She no longer sold drinks at her bar—she "exchanged" them for special tickets that were sold from the small apartment adjacent to the hall in which she lived.

Shortly after the conversion, the newly installed chief of police, Lemuel Ellsworth, paid an undercover visit to Johannesburg.

Dressed in a disguise of a rumpled suit and cheeky straw hat, Ellsworth bought a drink and faded into the mass of late-night revelers. What the chief saw confirmed to him that conditions at Rosina's were as bad as ever. Young people danced in tight, drunken pairs as a sloppy house band tooted out jaunty songs. All around him, beer and vulgar discussion flowed freely.

Patrons drinking at a Milwaukee dance hall
WHi Image ID 6510

But most alarming was the diversity of the writhing crowd—young girls and boys, married women, professional mashers, dashing rakes, pimps, loafers, and prostitutes. And mixed among all of these were African American men, talking and dancing with white women, sitting at their tables and buying them drinks. That night, amidst the revelry, Chief Ellsworth vowed from beneath his worn-out hat to do what no other city official had yet been able to do—he would end the party at Rosina's.

A week later, after yet another denial of a saloon permit for the place, Ellsworth struck. In the still of the hot summer night, he quietly trucked a small army of two dozen officers from the central station to Eighth and Galena. As the typical scene "of drunken debauchery and merriment" played out inside the hall, officers snuck into place, covering every door and window in the building. Just past midnight, Ellsworth's men burst in through the main and side doors. The crowd of more than one hundred was set into a panic and a stampede soon ensued. For a few precious moments, revelers managed to stream through a window left unguarded by the police. But the gap was quickly sealed, and Ellsworth's army aligned Rosina's patrons into two long lines and marched them out into the street. A pair of patrol wagons were filled to capacity and sent to the south-side and central stations. Those left behind were marched under guard to the nearby west-side station. In total, eighty-four men, women, and teenagers were taken in, each booked on a charge of being an inmate of a disorderly house.

Lost in the tumult of the raid was Rosina Georg. Always one for dodging the law, she had somehow managed to elude capture during the raid. While her patrons were booked en masse, a pair of detectives returned to the hall to search for her. She was found quickly, hiding in the attic of the building. Handcuffed and hauled to the west-side station, she was charged, yet again, with being the keeper of a disorderly house and operating a saloon without a permit.

The morning after the raid, five hundred people crowded into Market Square to gawk at those pulled during what was being called the biggest raid in city history. Newspapers marveled at the makeup of the prisoners. The *Sentinel* noted that the men taken in ranged from boys to old men, with "really every condition and class of life...represented." The paper described the women taken in as mostly between the ages of seventeen and twenty-five and consisting largely of the "daughters of the respectable German citizens of the north-western quarter of the city." The *Journal* found a bit more variety, writing that "women known to police circles wore an indifferent look [in court]," while "working girls, caught away from home, bedewed their handkerchiefs with emotion."

All but three of the arrested were convicted and fined five dollars. A pair of Irish women known as "professional rounders" and a young man with a bad reputation were each "sent to the works." Rosina pled not guilty and was released on three hundred dollars' bail, heading back home to continue running her dance hall. At her trial later that week, she presented her "private club" argument that supposedly freed Johannesburg from any city regulations. But the testimony by officers at the scene buried her. One claimed a majority of those in the place were under the age of fifteen. Another spoke of the young women and their dates—much older and with much darker complexions.

Just before the case went to the jury, attorney Austin made another attempt to have the licensing ordinance declared invalid, saying the language of the law in the official city books did not match the wording of the law the common council had passed. It turned out that Austin was right. For four days, city officials scrambled to determine if the mismatched law could still stand. During the delay, city attorney Robert Luscombe, long on the losing end of battles with Rosina, was heard to offer a bet of a box of cigars that his case was sunk. But, much to the chagrin of Rosina, the law was declared valid and Judge Mallory permitted the trial to continue. Rosina was found guilty and fined seventy-five dollars for the infraction—plus another seventy-five dollars for the charge of operating a saloon without a license that resulted from another arrest while she was out on bail.

The week after her conviction, Rosina made a show of renting her hall to a local temperance organization. A series of sparely attended meetings were held, with impassioned booze-fighters at the pulpit in the old dance room while her dedicated regulars sat secretly in the next-door barroom downing beer and whiskey. Shortly thereafter, a west-side brewery admitted to city officials that he had been supplying Rosina with two kegs of beer a week ever since her "conversion" to the cause of sobriety.

Worn weary by her battles with the city, Rosina sold her hall in August 1884 for four thousand two hundred dollars. The new owner said he intended on operating a saloon in the place, leading some to suspect the transaction was just another attempt by Rosina to get her permit. But she quickly made it clear that the deal was sincere. She had gotten married and was leaving the city, bound for Michigan to live nearer to family. Her husband, Conrad Stoll, had been a juror at her most recent trial. His was the last vote cast to convict. He "held out so long," the *Sentinel* wrote, "that the others threatened to have him sent up for perjury." Shortly after the wedding, she took Conrad to the courthouse to show him off to all the clerks and city officials with whom she had spent so much time. Asked if she wished to introduce him to city attorney Luscombe, she curtly declined. The happy couple left town a few days later.

RAIDS

April 1882

A T THE downtown central police station, police chief Robert Wasson organized his officers into ten six-man squads. All of the department's active manpower was about to partake in one of the largest raids in city history. For the next two hours, Milwaukee would effectively be without police protection, as the efforts of the force would be dedicated exclusively to "pulling" the occupants and customers of some of the most prominent brothels in the city. Just before 9:00 p.m., the men marched out into the warm spring night, quickly covering the few short blocks between the central station and Milwaukee's riverside red-light district.

Earlier in the day, a pair of undercover officers had made the rounds of the district, posing as out-of-towners in search of a high time. They did some quick bartering with the house madams and vowed to return that night. After their tour, the two officers went to a judge and swore out warrants against several houses of ill-fame. Wasson, who had been appointed to his post earlier in the month with the election of John Stowell as mayor, had planned the raid as the first in a series that would rid Milwaukee of the denizens of the district. First up to be pulled were the fine "sporting parlors" of River Street,[1] the rough west-of-the-river flophouse saloons of Second Street, and the notorious mixed-race dens of "Brown Row," located along the blocks of Wells Street nearest the river. As Wasson's army marched out into the streets that night, they were armed with warrants on fifteen different houses—no small order to be sure, but a mere fraction of the estimated ninety-five houses of prostitution operating in the city.

A view from the alley behind the notorious "Brown Row" of Wells Street

Historic Photo Collection / Milwaukee Public Library

---

1. Now Edison Street

By 10:30, the raids had left the central station "packed to suffocation." Outside, "the greatest confusion prevailed," as dozens of carriages and foot messengers flocked to the building, rushing bail money to the arrested and trying to account for brothel inmates caught up in the pull. In total, eighty-three people were hauled in, a number split almost equally between prostitutes and their male patrons. Most of the men were younger, typical of the nighttime downtown reveler. Among those pulled in were an unnamed deacon from a west-side Presbyterian church and an off-duty Illinois sheriff. One man brought in was an agent for a Boston brothel, most likely in town to arrange some kind of "transfer" for a sporting woman between the two cities. So eager was he to escape from Milwaukee, he was observed shouting in the crowded booking room that he would sell his $125 gold watch for the $30 cash to make bail. A bystander took him up on the offer and was admiring his new timepiece as the Bostonian made for the door. As was usual in raids of this type, most of the men arrested gave false names, paid their bail, and were never seen again.

The female arrestees were almost exclusively residents of the district. More than a dozen of the area's madams were pinched, including Miss Lizzie French, perhaps the city's most prominent brothel keeper. Of the working girls, many were already familiar with the police station's female quarters. Observing the scene, the *Milwaukee Sentinel* noted, "Some women cried, others laughed and made light of the matter, and still others uttered dire vengeance against the officers who arrested them."

By midnight, as the night-shift officers finally returned to their beats, all but about thirty-five of the arrestees had paid their bail, which totaled nearly two thousand dollars. Of those who could not raise the thirty dollars' bail, most were inmates of the bottom-rung Brown Row houses of Wells Street. By 2:00 a.m., the *Sentinel* reported, most of the houses pulled in the raid were back in operation, "although a little more careful in their admission."

PROTECTION
August 1884

PULLED IN during one of the increasingly commonplace raids
on the brothels of Milwaukee's downtown red-light district, Wells Street madam Fanny Seymour insisted to police
that her arrest was a mistake. She presented chief of police
Lemuel Ellsworth with a receipt that had been issued to her by
John McCallum, a local furniture dealer. It read, in part, that
McCallum had received ten dollars from Seymour, which was
"to be placed where it will do the most good in aiding or helping to keep the two blocks on Wells Street from being pulled
this year." The slip, Seymour insisted, was proof that she had
contributed to a pot of money that was to be split between Ellsworth and Mayor Emil Wallber to ensure that her part of the
district was not disturbed.

Seymour was one of at least three Wells Street keepers from
whom McCallum had solicited funds. He had come to them in
July 1884, shortly after Ellsworth and Wallber assumed their
offices. After a brief drive to clear out the district a few years
prior, the administration of Mayor John Stowell had mostly left
the brothels of Wells Street to their own devices. But Wallber
and his appointees had campaigned on reform. The fear that
they would make sport of the open brothel trade of the area
hung heavy that summer as McCallum started up his collection. He claimed to have a contact in City Hall who would, in
exchange for two hundred dollars that would be split between
Ellsworth and Wallber, ensure that the women of Wells Street
would not be pulled.

John McCallum was not a part of the regular scene in the
district. It was his furnishing firm that had outfitted the brothels of the street with draperies, chairs, sofas, and beds. He had
some twenty-five hundred dollars' worth of furnishings in these
houses, all being paid for in monthly installments. Should
these houses get pulled, his furnishing could be seized and his

debtors thrown out of work. Also in on the plan was Ben Weil, an agent for the property owners who rented to the madams. He represented a significant financial interest as well. At least six homes along Wells were leased from his client for purposes of prostitution, each bringing a monthly rent well above the going rate for the area. "Twice as much as the old shebangs are worth," in the words of one Wells Street madam.

But somewhere between collecting the money and getting it to Ellsworth and Wallber, McCallum's plan fell apart. He ended up using the cash to start a pot of funds to be held jointly by himself and Weir, an insurance fund on the monthly payments owed to each of them. And indeed, when the street got pulled, the two men dipped into the funds to keep their own ledgers current.

After the complaint made by Seymour, McCallum was arrested on a charge of obtaining money under false pretenses. Of the women who later came forward to admit they paid into his fund, most did not have much faith in the furniture man's ability to deliver on his claims. "I thought there was something crooked about it," Alice Fowler told the *Milwaukee Sentinel*. "If a couple hundred dollars were raised for McCallum's friend, why, we would be alright, d'ya see? Now, you know that's been [tried] before."

The *Sentinel* also went to Gypsy Howard, another Wells Street madam, and asked if she believed McCallum's claims. "Naw," she said between plumes of cigarette smoke. "At first, I thought there might be a little truth to the scheme. But, as soon as I heard what kind of a man Ellsworth was, I knew that our promised protection didn't amount to anything." She had not even bothered to save the receipt that McCallum had given her. "I felt like this—if Mr. McCallum wanted that ten dollars from me bad enough to work a game to get it, he was welcome to it."

Only Fanny Seymour seemed to have been a true believer in the plot. "Why, I thought we had a great snap when we paid our ten dollars," she told the *Sentinel*. "[And] I thought Ellsworth had a pile of gall after getting his little one hundred dollars to go back on his promise." She opined that she and her fellow Wells Streeters were targeted because the police "never got a smell" of the money McCallum raised. "Perhaps that's what they were sour about," she said with a laugh.

WITH BELLS ON
January 1922

T HE MOST recent fashion accessory of the Milwaukee "flapper" was causing concern among school officials in the city. Flappers—a teenaged "army of pretty little girls with bobbed hair, short skirts, and rouged faces," per the *Milwaukee Journal*—were known for their slinky sex appeal and alluring perfumes, but this new trend was drawing attention from more than just the eyes and nose. The most chic of the flapper set was now adorning her outfits with small, jingling bells "whose tinkle accommodates [her] promenade."

By the time these jingling flappers were set loose on summer vacation, the *Journal* was already declaring that the year 1922 would go down as that of the "great flapper controversy." "At 14, they look like grown women did before the war. At 17, they can pass for 24," the paper wrote. "If you are a high school boy, you say they have snap and make keen dates and you are proud to walk down the street with one of them hanging to your arm." Of course, it was not high school boys who were worrying so loudly about these girls and their "snap." The mobility and independence of the flapper seemed to some a fast road bound to ruin. Milwaukee flappers found idols at the movies and dressed to mimic their favorite female stars. They went with boys who drove fast cars, went to dance halls and roadhouses, and spent the money of their companions—or even their own, as many worked—on cold drinks and hot jazz. The *Journal* talked to one young girl who had just the night before been out until 3:00 a.m. at a country roadhouse. The reporter asked if there was any adult supervision to her night out. "What did we want of a chaperone?" the flapper spat. "We knew the boys, and anyway, a girl can take care of herself."

The reporter found another girl who was also familiar with the back roads. "Do boys take liberties with me? Not so you can notice," she told the man. "If I like a boy pretty well I let him kiss me if he wants to and, of course, he always wants to. If I don't like him, nothing doing." Seeing that the *Journal* man was taken aback by her attitude toward what was once a fairly verboten subject, she continued, "Why not? If you like boys, why not let them know it? Why not have a good time as you go along? There'll be trouble enough later on. Any movie will show you that."

Despite the somewhat shocking behavior the *Journal* man uncovered, he was less alarmed by the flapper than others. "So, why not let the flappers flap, if they want to?" he asked his readers. "Their momentary eccentricities probably are far more harmless than we choose to believe." As for the flappers' jingling dresses, school officials said they would probably move to ban bells from acceptable student clothing. The accompaniment, it was said, had a tendency to "distract the boy's attention from more serious matters."

V-GIRLS AND TROUBLE BOYS

July 1943

IN THE summer of 1943, Milwaukee County district attorney James Kerwin announced that the city of Milwaukee was "absolutely rotten" with "prostitution and carousing" and that the conditions bred by legal laxity against the wartime misdeeds of the city's youth were a "civic outrage." Kerwin said he was under considerable pressure from the federal government to clean up the city. He wanted funds to hire eight investigators to help bring the situation under control. He currently had only two men dedicated to the cause, and each was working in excess of fifteen hours per day. "The situation," he said, "is getting away from them."

The disruptions of the war years seemed to some to be causing Milwaukee's children to grow up much too quickly. A sharp
increase in tobacco and alcohol use among teens was reported by city officials. District judge Harvey Neelsen said that he
had seen more cases pertaining to underage drunkenness and
smoking during the spring of 1943 than he had in several pre-
war years combined. "Many business operators are under the
erroneous impression that they may legally sell cigarettes and
liquor to minors if the latter bring in notes signed by their parents," Neelsen said during the trial of a pharmacy clerk charged
with selling cigarettes to a thirteen-year-old boy. The boy had
provided the clerk with a note—written and signed by his thirteen-year-old friend—that granted "permission" for the transaction. The boys were later picked up by police puffing away in
Washington Park. They were turned over to their parents, to
whom the judge recommended a good "thrashing" for the boys.

Another recent case involved a thirteen-year-old girl who
procured four quarts of beer and a quart of wine from a West
Walnut Street tavern. The girl's mother arrived home from
work later in the day to find the girl and her three teenage
siblings quite drunk. An unnamed north-side tavern was alleged to have served a sixteen-year-old boy so much liquor that
he needed to be hospitalized. The previous March, a south-side
dive turned loose a boy of the same age so drunk that he passed
out in a snowbank, causing permanent damage to his arms and
legs.

With parents pulled from their houses in service of the war
effort, young people were often left to their own devices. It was
the eagerness of some to mimic the actions of their hard-living
elders that so alarmed Kerwin. But nothing was as startling as
the emergence in the city of the "v-girl." Shorthand for "victory
girl," the v-girl was a chaser of servicemen, a young woman or
girl who was said to have gone "khaki-wacky" by showing no
shame in making sexual advances toward soldiers and sailors.

Some v-girls came with a price, stalking the downtown bar-
rooms and dance halls in search of servicemen on liberty. A
sample of women arrested for prostitution during the war years
indicated as many as 60 percent of working v-girls were infected with venereal disease. Others were well practiced in the art
of "rolling," the act of getting a soldier drunk with liquor and
promises of sex, only to take him back to a designated apartment or hotel and rob him blind.

**A recently returned sailor and his admirers,
ca. 1943**
Library of Congress LC-USW3-038451-E, Lot 941

But even among the amateur v-girls, city officials found
much reason for concern. The man in uniform often attracted
the very young. Girls as young as thirteen were found by police in the company of soldiers in saloons and hotels. Lakefront
parks were particularly attractive spots for conspicuous lovers.
Over a single weekend in June 1945, police arrested eighteen
girls between the ages of thirteen and seventeen in Juneau

Park involved in some degree of intimacy with servicemen. Kerwin cited these cases as major reasons for the need for additional funds. He bemoaned the fact that many of the girls involved were let off with a mere "verbal spanking" and released to their parents.

Just days after Kerwin made his plea to the public, at least seven more underage girls were arrested for keeping company with soldiers and hauled to the juvenile detention center. A pair of sisters—identified in the *Milwaukee Journal* as Ruth, age fifteen, and Gladys, age thirteen (these were not their real names)—were taken by their mother to West Wells Street, paired off with two sailors, and dropped at Juneau Park. The only instruction their mother gave them was to "be home early." Cops picked up Gladys around midnight, waiting outside of a Wisconsin Avenue bar for her date to finish a round of drinks. They found Ruth shortly afterward, all finished with her fellow and walking home.

On the same night, police "had to interfere with the romance" of a fifteen-year-old girl lying in the grass with a serviceman. They chased the pair off with a warning, but when they found the same girl with a different man during a sweep of the park just over an hour later, they hauled her in. The girl lived with foster parents, who were out of town for the weekend. About an hour later, police nabbed girls of fourteen and sixteen saying good-bye to their most recent naval companions at the Lakefront Depot. The older of the two had been in the city for only two months. She was said to be living with a twenty-three-year-old woman with a "suspiciously fancy name" and bringing dates back to her downtown apartment. The fancily named woman was quickly arrested and held on unnamed charges.

Despite the urgency insisted by Kerwin, the County Board of Supervisors took a dim view of his request for additional officers. Citing the nationwide shortage of workers brought on the by war, they encouraged the district attorney to make due with what he had.

SPOONS

September 1926

"AUTOMOBILES WITH their freedom of restraint offer too much in the way of temptation," Reverend Harry Wise of the Milwaukee County Federation of Churches told the *Milwaukee Journal*. "If it's right to do at all, it should be done out in the open." The topic of the *Journal*'s inquiry was spooning—an act of youthful lovebirds that, according to the paper, involved "holding hands, an occasional hug, and perhaps one kiss each half hour." City church and school officials were becoming alarmed by the tendency of young people to engage in spooning in areas beyond the watchful eye of adults. These hidden hugs and covert kisses, it was feared, would lead to acts unfit for print. "Park benches are all right for spooning in the daytime, but at night? Well, there is some doubt in my mind as to their proper usage then," Wise continued. "If spooning, or courting, is done in the dark, sort of on the sly, away from the sight of anyone, I believe it is of doubtful propriety."

Reverend H. T. Fletcher of Kansas City had recently made news by opening a "spooning parlor" in his church and inviting young couples to embrace under the supervision of a congregation elder. Captain Harry McCoy, a detective with the Milwaukee Police Department, saw the spooning habit as a troubling trend but did not wish to see the Fletcher plan in his city. "In my opinion, nothing should be done to encourage spooning," McCoy told the *Journal*. "It is not the business of the church and it is certainly not up to the city to create cozy corners for courting." He felt they would do better to encourage young people to use such libidinous energies on outdoor sports.

Reverend Gustav Stearns was no more eager than McCoy to see spooning parlors in Milwaukee. Stearns preferred to see a permanent city commission created to combat the problem. "We have fish, game, and forest conservation commissions because we are scared to death of losing these things we like so well," he said. "I see no reason why we shouldn't pay at least as much attention to public morals." The *Journal* attempted to gauge the opinion of the city's flapper population—the group seemingly so much at risk—but their reporter could not find a single bob-headed girl willing to talk on the record of her habits of love.

The city had previously taken action on the matter of spooning in 1919, when the act was outlawed in canoes, citing a rash of complaints on young lovers paddling lightly near the resort district of the upper Milwaukee River. The ordinance even led to the purchase of the first motorboat used by the city police department, most appropriately christened the *Killjoy.*

"KILL THE KISS"
July 1912

"HOMES HAVE been wrecked, nations destroyed, thrones overturned, all because of that one thing," G. R. Bowling was quoted as saying in the *Milwaukee Sentinel.* Bowling was at the forefront of a movement in Oklahoma that several Milwaukee physicians were hoping to jump-start in Wisconsin. They were trying to ban "promiscuous osculation"—more commonly known as the kiss.

The anti-kissing charge in Milwaukee was led by Dr. L. A. Kleise, who won the support of several of his colleagues with a stirring oration against the practice at a city medical convention. "The habit is known to spread disease, not only when practiced on babies but with older persons as well," Kleise told the *Sentinel.* "I fear, however, that a law to this effect would be difficult to enforce."

The drive against the kiss was because of the germs the act was alleged to spread. "The kiss is a malady, like the whooping cough or the measles," said a physician opponent of the practice. "It is a blot on our civilization and should be dealt with drastically. I know of no better remedy than to have the proposed law passed and the policemen enforce it with a good hickory club if necessary."

Backers of the ban managed to get a bill before the state legislature for consideration. In the meantime, they vowed to take their fight to the public and conduct an investigation as to the opinion of the citizenry on the matter. They wished to avoid undue publicity which, they felt, could build a fast tide against their movement. Backers of the bill planned "lectures and literature to show the actual horrors and disease spreading tendencies in the apparently harmless and admittedly felicitous kiss."

Despite the odds against them, Milwaukee's anti-kiss crusaders felt confident about their cause. "In a few centuries, our grandchildren will look back and wonder how such a phase of insanity ever took hold of their progenitors," Kleise said. "Why must affection be shown by a salute of the lips? Why not run ears or noses or foreheads as they do in Africa? The slogan of the medical societies of America should be 'Kill the Kiss.'"

DIRTY BOOKS
December 1891

A WIDE-BODIED man of middle age, well dressed and adorned with a long, sweeping mustache, entered the Carl Caspar Antiquarian Bookstore at 437 East Water Street. The shop had a reputation as one of the city's finest. Its stock of rare books had been built by Caspar into one of world renown. The man with the mustache had never met Caspar, but in recent months, the two had done some business through the US mail. The man, who called himself Stewart, wished to see the stock of volumes that Caspar kept under lock and key. He wanted something hot.

Caspar trusted Stewart. His trading with the man previously had included a number of explicit photographs, mailed from Milwaukee to Stewart's home address in Chimney Point,

Vermont. Stewart examined Caspar's stock of illicit books and was impressed. He reasoned that they could be worth as much as a hundred and fifty to two hundred dollars a volume. But he was not there that day to make a purchase and left the shop in short order. As he walked off toward the police station, the man—whose real name was Anthony Comstock—could not get over the rare and filthy items he had just laid his hands on. He later said he was "mystified as to know how Caspar came into possession of [such rare books]."

Anthony Comstock was a native of Connecticut. He had an upbringing molded by the "fire and brimstone" religious fervor of his mother and swore off all impure thoughts from an early age. He fought for the Union in the Civil War and kept on fighting after the war ended. Gambling, tobacco, alcohol, and obscenity were among his targets. He gained a national reputation as the battling agent for the New York Society for the Suppression of Vice, championing the so-called Comstock Act of 1873 that forbade using the US mail to transport information on birth control or anything of an "obscene, lewd, or lascivious" nature. He was probably the nation's most recognizable name in the war on vice when he set Carl Caspar in his sights.

Through methods never detailed, Comstock became aware that Caspar was dealing in what Comstock considered to be obscene material. As a volunteer inspector for the US Postal Service, Comstock often personally investigated individuals he believed to be violating his namesake law. To bust Caspar, he acquired a mailing address in the little town of Chimney Point, Vermont, and wrote the bookseller asking for a list of stock. After trading correspondence for a time to build a sense of trust, Comstock asked for a stock of his more "illicit" volumes. Caspar complied, sending a handwritten account of what he could offer. Sometime in the latter half of 1891, Comstock— writing as "Stewart"—ordered a small number of photographs of an explicit nature. Caspar wrote that he preferred to send them via a privately run express company, but Comstock wrote back that his little town had no express office, and travel to the nearest such office was prohibitive. Caspar relented and dropped the photos in the mail. A few months later, Comstock arrived in Milwaukee to finish the sting.

Caspar was arrested and charged in federal court with violation of the Comstock Act. The next month, he went to trial, with Comstock eager to testify against him. The newspapers viewed his methods in the case with a jaundiced eye. The *Milwaukee Journal* wrote that the "great apostle of morality...played a very sharp trick on the bookseller." The judge in the case took a similar stance, saying that Comstock "may be able to reconcile such conduct to the laws of God and morality, but this court cannot." Caspar, in his own defense, claimed to have not known what he did was a crime. He assumed the sale of such material—to be used by private individuals for no "immoral purposes"—was within the bounds of the law. The judge dismissed such a defense, but even in accepting Caspar's eventual guilty plea, took another slap at Comstock. "There are some things worse than sending obscene materials through the mails," he said. "Lying by a government official [is] worse." The judge handed Caspar a five-hundred-dollar fine, which the bookseller paid on the spot. He told the court that he would destroy any obscene material that remained in his possession at the first opportunity.

PEPPY TALES

April 1941

A T 6:30 on a Friday evening, a small squad of vice officers and assistant district attorneys rushed through the front door of the Hurwitz Bookstore at 2436 West Vliet Street. After securing the place, the officers rushed about two miles to 518 West State Street, where they similarly pulled the Century Bookstore. On Vliet, police placed sixty-one-year-old Leo Hurwitz under arrest. On State, they cuffed Harry Hurwitz, Leo's twenty-four-year-old son. The charge was the possession and sale of obscene material: photos, magazines, and paperbacks containing images and illustrations of nudity, salacious stories, and vividly detailed content on sexual hygiene. Among the titles of the five thousand volumes seized were *Sexology, Bedtime Tales, Real Tempting Tales, Parisienne,* and *Gay Life.* Each of the seized items was kept hidden behind the counter and was not in open view of shoppers. To get these items, someone needed to know enough to ask for them specifically. Police noted that the typical cover price on the items was just twenty-five cents, "within the purchasing power of high school youth."

Police executed the raids after a series of complaints from parents of children who attended schools near the stores. It was only the second such action ever undertaken by county officials, the first having occurred in 1938 against another bookstore operated by a son of Leo Hurwitz. Both actions occurred under the supervision of Milwaukee County district attorney Herbert Steffes. It was Steffes himself who led the raiders at both the Vliet and State locations. The day after the Hurwitzes' arrests, Steffes and his assistant, Charles Kersten, appeared in a staged photo in the *Milwaukee Sentinel.* Among dozens of bundles of seized girlie books, Steffes was shown examining a copy of *Lu-Lu Magazine* as Kersten nervously looked on.

Eight weeks later, the Hurwitzes went on trial. Kersten, acting as prosecutor on the case, read aloud to the jury a story titled "Maizie Paid the Balance" from a paperback copy of *Peppy Tales,* one of the volumes seized in the raids. Defense attorney Arthur Richter countered by reading passages from Shakespeare, claiming the material contained in the "Maizie" tale and the other seized property was no more offensive than what he had just read. "We are not judging literature," Kersten retorted. "What we are considering is this trash seized from a bookstore. Placing this in the hands of adolescents is dynamite. It will lead to sex crimes."

With the emphasis of the prosecution's case firmly planted in the alleged—yet unproven—availability of the material to minors, Richter aimed his closing statement directly at the young, wavy-haired Kersten. "Mr. Kersten would have you believe that you are here to protect the morals of some curly headed boy," Richter said. "The only curly headed boy you are being asked to protect is a professional snooper from the district attorney's office. The state has not proved a single sale to a minor."

It took the jury of three men and three women less than an hour to bring back guilty verdicts for the Hurwitzes. Despite having the option to simply fine the two men, Judge A. J. Hedding handed each a four-month jail sentence. "We must send out a message," Hedding said, "that will stop purveyors of obscene literature in their tracks." Mayor Frank Zeidler strongly supported the verdict, saying publically after the trial, "If it were in my power to send a garbage truck up to some of these stands and then dump their loads into the incinerator, I would be glad to do so."

ORGY AT THE WORKHOUSE
March 1934

A COUNTY board investigation into graft, corruption, and cruelty at the Milwaukee County House of Corrections and Workhouse revealed a slate of wrongdoings at the facility. The place mostly held men and women convicted on minor state charges, but during Prohibition it also housed those convicted on federal bootlegging charges. Chief among the complaints was the allegation that the favor of authorities at the facility was readily available for purchase. Guards were known to sell whiskey and marijuana to prisoners who could get money from friends or family. Armin Kreutzer, a Milwaukee veterinarian convicted of performing abortions, was accused of having bribed his way into being allowed to leave the prison grounds to continue his illicit practice. One prisoner allegedly received a new suit of clothes from a guard in exchange for a tryst with the prisoner's wife. Another was supposedly allowed to leave the grounds to host lavish all-night parties at the downtown

Randolph Hotel—to which many prison officials were invited.

Most stunning among the allegations leveled during the investigation were those from Lillian Larson, sent twice to the house of corrections on charges of running a brothel. Larson detailed mistreatment and favoritism in the women's wing of the facility. Some prisoners were given bare-bones rations while the "privileged girls" ate handsomely. According to Larson, privileges came at a steep price but allowed for incredible freedoms. "One girl, her name was Pauline, told me she paid twenty-five dollars a month for privileges," Larson testified in an unusually full hearing room. "Her husband called Sunday and her sweetheart called in the evening. The girl told me she was allowed to stay three hours in a room alone with her sweetheart." She spoke of other privileged women allowed morphine and needles to feed their addictions. She said that privileged girls were never punished, but those unable to make monthly payments were severely reprimanded, often physically, for slight infractions.

One item in Larson's testimony managed to make national news. It was the story of a New Year's Eve party held in the women's wing in either 1928 or 1929. The privileged girls were allowed out of their cells and permitted to call in their husbands, boyfriends, or lovers for the evening's festivities. The climax of the party, quickly dubbed an "orgy" by the press, resulted in one inmate dancing through the halls of the cell block stark naked, pouring drinks for the unprivileged girls, who remained locked in their cells, all while the matron of the wing slumped stone drunk in a chair. During Larson's salacious story, several men, both civilian bystanders and county officials, were asked to leave the room as they could provide no reason why the young woman's testimony was in any way related to their duties.

After several weeks of testimony, county officials relieved the facility's superintendent, William Momson, of his duties and the Milwaukee County sheriff took control of the jail.

"A SPECULATIVE MOOD"
July 1872

T HE *MILWAUKEE SENTINEL* reported on a man who, with "some old burgundy [in] the head," enjoyed an early Independence Day celebration. After becoming quite drunk in a downtown saloon, the man found himself in a very generous mood. He loudly proposed purchasing the Franklin House hotel so that he might use it to entertain his friends—who were, no doubt, quite numerous at the moment. He said that he might also purchase the old city hall, officially known as Market Hall, at East Wells and North Water. Since the city had just transferred its offices into the county courthouse, he reasoned he could outfit the place with a bar and billiard tables. As these transactions could not be immediately secured, he started throwing about smaller sums of cash. He offered ten dollars for a "pint of pea nuts." He wagered one hundred dollars with a man that Horace Greeley would win the upcoming presidential election (Greeley lost) and bet yet another stranger fifty dollars that he was not intoxicated (he was, quite). It was not reported if he secured the "pea nuts" or if he was called on to pay up for either of the two bets. Police finally interceded on the man's spree when he smashed the lamps of a hack driver's carriage. When the man was booked at the station, a wad of fifteen hundred dollars in cash was found in his pocket. "A night's carousal in Milwaukee," noted the *Sentinel*, "especially in his princely mood, might have dissipated his cash as overindulgence had his prudence."

PAJAMAS
December 1932

H ARRY MOORE might have been the only speakeasy keeper in Milwaukee who worked in his pajamas. He ran a small operation out of an apartment on the second floor of a building at 113 East Wells Street, along a stretch of downtown known as Gin Alley. The costuming was a safety mechanism against a possible raid by local dry agents. When Moore heard a knock at the door, he shuffled toward it and cracked it open. If he did not recognize the faces he saw, he yawned and said in his sleepiest of voices, "What do you mean by waking up an honest citizen at this time of night?" But when a pair of federal agents with a warrant on his place showed up one winter night, the just-out-of-bed act failed to convince them. They shoved past the pajama-clad keeper and quickly uncovered his small nightspot. The feds seized his stash and arrested Moore and his bartender. Both men faced a night in jail. Moore was already dressed for it.

DARKNESS IN THE BADLANDS
January 1931

F ROM ALL over the Midwest, sixty agents of the US Treasury Department's Prohibition unit crept toward Milwaukee. They were about to help execute the biggest liquor raid in the history of one of the nation's most alcohol-soaked cities. The next afternoon, the visiting feds—joined by fifteen local agents—congregated downtown. Led by Wisconsin's Prohibition Office deputy administrator W. Frank Cunningham, the agents broke into squads of two or four, with each squad receiving the address of a known Milwaukee speakeasy. Each spot included in the raid had a corresponding federal warrant accusing its proprietors of violating the Volstead Act, the federal law that outlawed the sale and transportation of intoxicating beverages.

At 5:30 p.m., Cunningham's army struck in unison, "like lightning out of a clear sky," in the words of the *Milwaukee Sentinel,* rushing through inconspicuous, unmarked doorways and the backrooms of a score of front shops and offices. The synchronized strike disarmed the old "tip-off" system usually employed by such places, the phone chain between friendly saloon keepers to warn the next stop down the street about the impending raid. The *Sentinel* reported of one such call attempted to an alleged seafood restaurant at 437 West State Street. "Lemme talk to Jimmie," said the man whose place was being raided.

"This is Jimmie," answered the voice at the end of the line.

"Don't sound like yer voice, Jim. But anyways, listen, there's about a million feds workin.' Close up the joint."

"That'd been a swell idea about an hour ago," replied the grinning Prohibition man on the line before hanging up.

It was all over in two hours, with twenty-six dens raided and thirty-eight men and women in custody on federal charges. "A terrific governmental punch at Milwaukee night life," the *Sentinel* proclaimed. Of the twenty-six places hit, twenty-two were concentrated in a five-block-by-four-block pocket of downtown, running from Clybourn to State and between the Milwaukee River and Fifth Street. The arrestees were a familiar bunch and proved to be a "colorful and noisy" mass of prisoners. They quickly took up a chant, demanding "Bail! Bail! Bail!" but the Prohibition agents were not moved. The group remained in jail for the evening and, in the morning, was hauled en masse to the Wisconsin Avenue federal building for arraignment.

With so many of the pinched in such close quarters, it did not take long to surmise who was to blame for such a well-executed raid. For three months in late 1930, a man known as Brad Bradley was a regular visitor to many of the targeted nightspots. Presenting himself as a safety match salesman, Bradley was actually an undercover federal agent, tasked with collecting information and swearing out warrants against places where illegal liquor was being sold. Bradley arrived, in the words of the *Sentinel*, "a stranger in the city, with a suave, confident manner." He quickly won the trust of Milwaukee operators, spending freely and drinking as one of the boys. The nature of his business—matches were something saloon proprietors typically supplied to their patrons—allowed him to embed himself with his targets, collecting names, addresses, and other information for potential sales leads. Among the same company where he was once "greeted as a Good Time Charlie," he was now cursed in the most vile terms. But their "Bradley" was by then in a different city, using a different name and most likely winning the confidence of a new group of hard-luck barkeeps.

The Milwaukee County Jail at the corner of Broadway and Wells, where the men pulled in during a federal raid waited for bail
Historic Photo Collection / Milwaukee Public Library

In the wake of the raid, the typically pulsating heart of Milwaukee's Badlands was dark and still. "Sadness will reign [tomorrow] in the hearts of Milwaukee's tipplers," the *Sentinel* wrote, "for many a haven for the weary is closed." A reporter for the paper observed the quiet street, occasionally visited by "a few derby hatted customers" who had not gotten news of the raid. They would try the trick doors at their favorite spots, like "the [Wells Street] blanket shop that hasn't sold a blanket since it opened," and get no reply. These men would keep trying doors until they got the idea, or until a passerby told them about Cunningham's raid. In a place with about twelve hundred "soft drink parlors" listed in the city directory, it was unlikely those put out in the Badlands needed to travel far to slake their thirst.

BLACK JACK

August 1881

A STORY was being circulated in the city of a well-to-do local farmer whose wife had become hopelessly addicted to opium. Unable to stop her from using the drug, the farmer locked her in a small room in their house, hoping time could cure her insatiable habit. After several days of confinement, the farmer finally allowed the poor woman to leave the room. She snuck away at the soonest chance and headed for the city, where she broke into several general stores, stealing items and reselling them to secondhand stores, before taking her cash to the nearest opium den. She was found sometime later and was, according the *Milwaukee Sentinel*, "stupefied by [opium] and in blissful ignorance of her surroundings."

Milwaukee's troubles with opium dated back to pioneer times, when its most regular users were the elderly. By 1880, when the *Sentinel* sent a reporter to investigate use of the drug in the city, they reported that most users had already died off. But rumors abounded of prominent and wealthy residents partaking of the drug. Opium use was most commonly associated with the Chinese, but the reporter found that use among that race in the city was limited. Overall, women were three times more likely to use opium than men and its use was most concentrated in the "pitiful class of abandoned women." Few users smoked the stuff, the reporter learned, with men more likely to eat it and women preferring to dilute it in hot water and "sip it as they would tea." Some turned to opium to ease physical pain or to soothe mental troubles, while others used it for "its stimulating and happy effect."

A similar inquest the following year found the opium trade in the city to be centered in the Badlands of the Fourth Ward. A *Sentinel* man visited one such den in the basement of a bakery and candy shop at 276 Third Street. The Ring Shane Laundry provided a front for the den, which was run by a dope boss known only as Sam, who had arrived in the city from New Orleans four months earlier. The "forbidding and noisome" quarters of the place were filthy and hot, strewn with trash and dirty clothes. A room off of the main area was provided for those who wished to smoke their dose, which sold at wholesale values for between eight and ten dollars per pound. Unlike the assertions the paper had made the year before, it now reported the trade to be growing. The city health department was investigating several low-end pharmacies that also sold "vast" amounts of opium, along with an increasing volume of morphine. "The evil," the *Sentinel* wrote, "is assuming vast and terrible proportions."

"NOW, I DON'T CARE."

September 1934

S HERIFF JOSEPH SHINNERS and two deputies hid in the shadows at the Chicago Road Inn in Milwaukee's southwestern corner. A car approached and one of its three occupants exited. He carried a small tin of opium, a delivery for Joyce Elmore, the roadhouse's twenty-seven-year-old proprietor and an admitted addict. Elmore had been arrested in downtown Milwaukee just days earlier. In exchange for leniency, she agreed to help the police pull down one of the several Chinese-run opium dens in the city. Out on bond, she called a contact at a Fourth Street Chinese boardinghouse and placed an order. Before the tin reached Elmore's hands, Shinners and his men leapt from hiding spots and nabbed twenty-six-year-old George Moy, placing him under arrest on a narcotics possession charge. Also pinched were Toy Bong and Frank Sam, who waited in the car as Moy made the delivery.

All three gave a home address of 939 Fourth Street. Police quickly moved on the building, which had been operating ostensibly as a rooming house and laundry. Police discovered a large room equipped with gaming tables and gambling machines hidden behind a small lobby. They found a similar setup in the basement, where detectives arrested a large group of Chinese men playing cards. The upper floor was divided into small rooms, each containing a hard bed and a small table. These were the rooms, police alleged, where addicts would smoke, eat, or inject opium. At the rear of the upper floor was a kitchen, stocked with cartons of rice, noodles, and other Chinese foods. Police arrested forty-seven people and seized five jars of opium pills, three jars of opium prepared for smoking, and a variety of associated paraphernalia. The total value of the drugs found was about three hundred dollars. They also uncovered evidence of an extensive lottery operation. They found a large cache of ticket receipts, which they believed represented payouts made to gamblers, along with a poster of Chinese charters detailing how the ten- to fifty-cent buy-in could result in top prizes of a thousand dollars.

Elmore told police that operations like this were running from several locations in the Chinese district of the city. This was at least the second time Elmore had helped in the raid of an opium den. In 1928, busted under the assumed name of Cecilia Burlick, she tipped cops off on a Wells Street den that resulted in a raid and several arrests. Elmore herself had a long history with the drug. "I was fifteen years old when I ran away from my home here to Chicago with a boyfriend," she told the *Milwaukee Journal* from her jail cell, locked away on the charge of being a habitual user of narcotics. "I obtained a job as a hostess in a night club. My friend used morphine. I started to use it because it kept my spirits high and my eyes bright. That was an asset in my work."

By 1934, Elmore walked with a pronounced shuffle, and her face showed her years of hard living. Locked away from her typical doses, her hands trembled as she spoke. "Morphine became too expensive, so I turned to opium," she said. "In Chicago, opium is easy to get and not very costly. At first I only needed one shot a day, but now I need at least four. I knew it was licking me, but I was powerless to fight it off. I tried the reduction cure several time, but it was no use. Now, I don't care."

After her 1928 arrest, Elmore was committed to the asylum at Waupun and held for five months. She was declared cured but quickly returned to her old ways. She used by pricking a hole in her skin, applying a drop of opium to the open wound, and then covering it with iodine. Matrons at the jail said that her legs resembled "corduroy cloth." She complained of severe bone aches and feared reprisal from those whom she turned over. "You know what happens to stool pigeons," she told the *Journal*. The newspaper reported that she was "on the verge of hysteria."

Meanwhile, federal narcotics agents arrived in the city from Chicago to investigate the Fourth Street den and its operators on drug, gambling, and human trafficking charges. Agents reported that Milwaukee had become a hub for opium and marijuana distribution throughout the Midwest. They investigated claims that airplanes, stocked with drugs, had landed at Curtiss-Wright Airport[1] and were met by leaders of a local Chinese narcotics ring. As the sensational claims of the feds made headlines, Jack King (sometimes referred to as Jack Hing), operator of a Chinese importing firm just a few doors from the Fourth Street den, pressed for those arrested in the raid to

---

1. Now Timmerman Field

be released. King claimed that there was no organized gambling in the neighborhood and that those in the boardinghouse had no idea of the drugs on the premises. The community was too poor to gamble, King said. Those seen playing cards in the basement, he claimed, had been playing for buttons.

No charges came from the most sensational of the claims aimed at Milwaukee's Chinese American community. In October 1934, Elmore was sentenced to six months to a year in jail but eventually agreed to undergo a voluntary treatment program at a federal prison in West Virginia. George Moy, the bagman lured into arrest at Elmore's roadhouse, was given one to two years in jail, but the sentence was suspended due to his otherwise clean record. Of the forty-seven arrested during the raid, forty-three were charged with being inmates of a disorderly house, pled guilty, and were freed after paying a one-dollar fine.

FROM CHICAGO
May 1866

THOMAS RYAN, a young man with a pronounced physical disability and without the means to support himself, was brought before a judge on a charge of vagrancy. Asked how he happened to find himself in Milwaukee without a place to stay, a job to work, or business to conduct, he confirmed what many in the city had suspected for some time. He said that he had come from Chicago. He arrived in Milwaukee after being forced onto a northbound train by men acting on behalf of either the city or the railroads. Chicago, it seemed, was shipping its homeless to Milwaukee. Judge James Mallory pledged an investigation into the matter. "It would be well for the railroad men to bear in mind," he said, "that the statutes impose a severe penalty for transporting vagrants into the state."

The arrival of Chicago's undesired had become a near-daily occurrence and would persist as an issue throughout the summer, causing the police department to take aggressive actions.

The *Sentinel* reported on a man arrested a few weeks later for wandering near the Walker's Point Bridge "with no apparent object in view." When the arresting officer insisted the man come with him to the central station, the man refused, saying he would only go along if he was taken to a first-class hotel, as he stayed at no other kind. Finally, the officer "convinced" him to go along and charged the man with vagrancy. ANOTHER CONTRIBUTION FROM CHICAGO, the headline read.

While most of those arrested for vagrancy were transient men, the most prominent of the street dwellers of this time was likely Margaret Williams, who racked up some two dozen arrests during her short time in the city. In early July, she was picked up and given her usual sixty days under lock and key. "Another of the low vagrants who infest the city," the *Sentinel* said of her.

Two Chicago men were arrested a few weeks later after being caught begging door-to-door. One of the men was missing a hand. Still, the *Sentinel* noted that "he might work if he tried with the other—he appeared too lazy to try." The men were convicted and given ninety days in jail with the usual vagrancy caveat that their sentence would be waived if they left the city. It was not reported whether they entered the care of the county or left for the next town.

Some more of Chicago's suspected deposits in the city were picked up a few weeks later when two teenaged girls were arrested early one morning rambling through the Third Ward, causing a "great annoyance to the peaceable conditions of the ward." The girls could give no account of themselves and had been "insulting the passersby with the filthiest language." The next day, a man named Foley, nabbed by police for begging, was given two months at the county poor farm. "His dress consists of a coat of many colors," the *Sentinel* noted, "and an even greater number of holes."

The most disturbing trend of the summer, however, proved to be a peculiar sport of the men who loafed about the downtown area. A small number of them had made a game out of "ejecting from their filthy mouths streams of tobacco juice upon the dresses of ladies who happen[ed] to be passing near them." The spitters tried to perform the act without being detected, but police and the newspapers could only guess as to the aims of such action. The *Sentinel* expressed hope that "good fortune may favor some man to witness the performance of this insult and outrage and visit promptly upon the offender that justice which should be meted to so cowardly a villain."

The outrage over northbound vagrants faded after 1866, suggesting Judge Mallory's inquest had some success. Margaret Williams, however, remained a regular entry in court registers for the next two years before fading from the record. A notable arrest in 1867 found her "so drunk as to be unable to navigate the streets without frequently coming to a halt at full length on the pavement or in the gutter." In August 1868, she was released from a jail stay only to be arrested again the next week and given ninety days in the house of corrections. She told the *Sentinel* that upon her next release, she hoped to leave the city and never return. The newspaper expressed the same hope.

THE OLD MOTHER'S HOUSE
August 1858

WILLIAM WARNKE was well known along the rugged dirt road known as Northeast Water Street.[1] His mother, Catherine, ran one of the many brothel houses for which the eastern bank of the Milwaukee River was notorious. He was making his way back to the house one Sunday night, in his typical drunken state, when he grabbed the arm of a passing woman and tried to drag her into his mother's den of ill-repute. It was never reported why Warnke grabbed her—the *Milwaukee Sentinel* described him as having committed an "insult" to the woman—but she was frightened enough to resist with a

---

1. Now East Water Street

fury. She managed to pull away from him and was about to run off when he raised the glass pitcher he had for some reason been carrying and threatened to smash the item over her head. The sounds of the struggle and the screams of the woman alerted the neighbors, and a mob of local men and boys quickly surrounded the drunk and his glass weapon. The crowd administered a "sound drubbing" to the man before turning their rage toward "Old Mother" Warnke's brothel.

The place had been a point of neighborhood consternation for some time. Police had raided the operation twice that month, handing Warnke convictions for keeping a house of ill-fame each time. But the Old Mother had built up a considerable fortune by trading in flesh. She paid her one-hundred-dollar fines almost without thought and, in the words of the *Sentinel*, "continued in her wicked course quite defiant of the law."

Feeling no protection from the statute books, the residents of the block decided to take up matters for themselves. The crowd rushed into the house, smashing out its windows and doors as the Old Mother's stable of young women fled into the street. The mob stripped the walls bare and reduced its fine furnishings to rubbish. They might have burned the place to the ground had the police not arrived on the scene and ordered them to disperse. The Old Mother and her son were arrested, as was another woman who helped run the place, identified in the *Sentinel* only as "Old Sib, wife of Spencer the Murderer." The police claimed the arrests were made as much to protect the trio from the still-simmering mob as anything else.

The next day in court, it seemed that the entirety of Water Street had turned out to get a look at the Warnke gang. The Old Mother was the star attraction, described by the *Sentinel* as a "hoary old sinner, being between 50 and 60 years of age." She was charged yet again with being the keeper of a house of ill-fame and had her bail set at the lofty sum of a thousand dollars—almost twice the average American's yearly salary. The *Sentinel* reported much rejoicing within the courtroom when the Old Mother, unable to raise the cash, was led off to jail.

Later that week, Old Sib and William Warnke were convicted on similar charges and ordered to pay a twenty-five-dollar fine or leave the city. The Old Mother was also convicted and fined an undisclosed amount. She opted to pay up, stay in the city, and continue on in her "wicked course."

RIVER STREET RIVALS

August 1875

"THE CONDUCT of the bawds of River Street has reached a state of notoriousness that deserves the immediate attention of the police," wrote the *Milwaukee Sentinel*. The "River Street" the paper referred to was not just the little four-block road that ran along the east bank of the Milwaukee River but rather the half mile square around the street that had become home to dozens of brothels and was thick with "pimps, loafers, and prostitutes." The *Sentinel* made this declaration after another one of the area's many vicious rows. In this case, the combatants were Alice Jordan and Susan Fuller, madams who ran competing houses along the same block. A fistfight between the women drove Fuller to swear out a warrant on Jordan on battery charges. Jordan was arrested, and the next day, Fuller appeared before a judge to make her case. But the judge found the evidence lacking, tossed the charges, and ordered Fuller to pay all associated court costs.

But even as the law was finished with the matter, Jordan could not so easily forget. Enraged that Fuller had caused her arrest, she waited for the woman after the proceedings and thrashed her with a parasol in the hallway outside the courtroom. The attack sent Fuller flying back into the judge's chambers, demanding that yet another warrant be taken out on Jordan for battery. The judge initially declined to act, but eventually complied at the insistence of Moses Fuller, Susan's husband.

With her arrest now pending, Jordan returned home to River

Street, still stewing over the matter. That night, she sought out Fuller and revealed to her that several times during the preceding months, she had accompanied Moses on long and intimate carriage rides through local "summer gardens." Fuller flew into a fury and stormed to Jordan's brothel house, where she took out her wrath on the glassware—destroying every window, lamp, drinking glass, and bottle of booze in the place. "The rage of the woman," the *Sentinel* reported, "knew no bounds."

The next day, both Jordan and Fuller were arrested on the grounds that they were idle persons with no visible means of support, a catchall charge used to round up vagrants and others found undesirable by the police. Within hours, they were convicted and each sentenced to ninety days at the house of corrections. Both women, the *Sentinel* wrote, "resolve to enter upon honorable and useful courses upon the expiration of their imprisonment."

MASHERS
May 1881

IN A story recounted in a letter to the *Milwaukee Sentinel*, two schoolgirls were walking through the downtown shopping district early one evening when they became aware they were being followed by a pair of young men. One of these "well-dressed scoundrels" approached the girls and, after an apology for intruding, asked if he and his friend might walk the girls home. He claimed to know something about the "reputation" of the girls. The girls became terrified and rushed home with quickened steps as the two young rakes trailed behind. The father of one of the girls, the letter said, was "perambulating the streets with vengeance depicted in his countenance and a rawhide in his coat sleeve."

This insult upon the girls was the work of "mashers," young male flirts who threw their affections at female passersby in the main commercial districts of the city. The look of the masher was one meant for an unmistakable indication of his intentions. "He wears a jaunty little hat on one side of his head," the *Sentinel* wrote, "grasps a slender cane, and always carries the paraphernalia of his guild in the shape of showy handkerchiefs, buttonhole bouquets, and other fascinating and fancy trifles." By early evening, the paper claimed, the streets were so thick with such "brutish-looking and fantastical apes" dressed in the "very latest agony" that women could not venture out unaccompanied without being subjected to their "insults."

A flirt and two ladies near the Milwaukee River
WHi Image ID 105457

The typical habit of these "dainty darlings of the dive" was to "sally forth" beginning in the late afternoon along downtown's Grand Avenue and Broadway. Finding a pretty girl, the masher would follow a few paces behind. Once he was confident she had no male companion nearby, he would quicken his pace and begin his pitch. But these lifted hats and blown kisses of the masher usually had no effect on the more respectable women of the city. "They do not reap much of a harvest," the *Sentinel* claimed, "until after the supper is over, the dishes are cleared, and the housework done up—when the cooks, servants, and chamber maids come out to have flirtations with their social vis-à-vis."

If one was caught on the mash, an arrest and fine could follow. The same day the letter to the *Sentinel* told of the angry father on the hunt for the insulters of his daughter, it was reported that a young Milwaukee man had been convicted of "professional mashing" for following a "respectable" girl to her house and throwing unwanted kisses in her direction. A fine of twenty dollars was assessed. He still may have fared better than the masher reported on a week earlier, who had the misfortune of approaching a woman outside a Broadway music store as her husband, an unnamed county official, was inside. Spying the young rascal through the door, he chased him from the scene, knocked him down, and gave him a sound thrashing.

Writing with a decidedly alarmist tone—one article was titled "KILL THE MASHER"—the *Sentinel* noted that summer was very near and that soon the mashers at the lakefront parks would be "as thick as gnats at a country cowyard." The problem, the paper asserted, would get worse before it got better.

SECRETS

THERE ARE SOME things a city will not share. As Milwaukee spread out from the nexus of its riverways, its dark places multiplied. These hidden corners—of muddied streets, quiet rooms, and troubled minds—keep secrets still. These are stories that cannot be completed: stories of liars whose creations were both purposeful and senseless, faceless killers possessed of the devil's luck and never brought to answer for their deeds, and occurrences so strange that their mere retelling seems to be its own kind of lie.

Then, as now, the impulse was to solve these mysteries, unmask the hoaxsters, and settle the balance of what our eyes see and our minds assume. But in their incomplete state, these stories achieve a different kind of wholeness. Their gaps reflect a city's imperfect understanding of itself. Their gaps memorialize a history that will never be complete.

The city has witnessed things that we can never know. In its darkened rooms, behind its locked doors, and in the frigid hug of rivers and lake, these stories unfold in simple actions lost to history but in plain view of the places we still occupy. That Milwaukee bore witness to these unknowns links the victims, killers, liars, and ghosts to this place. And just as this place keeps these secrets, it keeps others, and it keeps ours—all residents in a population of things-left-unknown that will never be brought to account.

THE VANISHERS

February 1935

A N AVERAGE of three Milwaukeeans were reported missing per day in the midst of the Great Depression. About 95 percent of these people were later located safe and sound—their "disappearances" typically the result of anxious loved ones prematurely contacting authorities. The other 5 percent, however, comprised the sad, the gruesome, and the cunning. Some were eventually found dead: of natural causes, accidents, or the unfortunate few murdered by their own hand or that of another. But some simply seemed to have been blown away with the lake winds. Some met an awful fate that prevented their recovery. And still more disappeared intentionally, those who "succeed in masking their identities [and] breaking with their old [lives]."

Some fled for financial reasons. The world economic state fed this, driving men from the wives and children they could not support and forcing idle workers to search for more fruitful surroundings. But occasionally, an excess of finances caused Milwaukeeans to skip town without notice. Clerks, accountants, and other people with access to—and having taken liberties with—the cash accounts of their employers often split at the first indication of suspicion. In the summer of 1934, a bottle was found on the beach near North Point with a note that read, "When you find this, I will be at the bottom of Lake Michigan. Good by [*sic*]." Police later found the man who had signed the note "alive, well, and repentant." He had been embezzling from his employer for some time.

Men were more likely to break away than women, with missing males outnumbering females two-to-one. "Nagging and scolding wives are of the main things that send Milwaukee men into hiding," noted the all-male Milwaukee Police Department. Males also ran off at a younger age than females, the typical age of missing boys being between seven and nineteen, and that of girls somewhere between fourteen and twenty-one.

When a woman went into hiding, police generally found it easier to ascertain from the missing's friends what had driven her from the city. Males were more likely to keep their motives to themselves. When a woman fled, she did so most likely "in search of excitement." Police Captain Frank Prohaska said that most thrill-seeking women were later found in Chicago, "living in poverty, full of despair, and ready to accompany detectives back to Milwaukee."

For those of whom no account could be made, an open file was kept. "Until our investigation proves otherwise," Prohaska said, "every missing adult person is regarded either as a victim of foul play or having taken their own life." The police kept a list, as old as the department itself, with the names of all open cases. No one was struck from the list until he or she turned up—dead, living, or otherwise.

THE RUNAWAYS
September 1898

ON A street corner near the Wells Street train depot in Chicago, two Milwaukee children approached a police officer. "Take us to our Uncle Adam," John Matthews, age ten, told the cop. At his side was his eight-year-old sister, Louisa. When the officer told the kids he had no idea who Uncle Adam was, John offered an alternative. "Well, take us to our Aunt Polly then."

The pair ended up at the police station. When asked how they had come to be so far from home, John told the police they had been kidnapped. According to the boy, the pair had been approached at Milwaukee's Chicago and North Western railroad depot—"the big house by the lake," as he put it—by a well-dressed woman who asked them if they would like to take a train ride. They said they would and she purchased three tickets, loaded them aboard a southbound train, and sat with them all the way to Chicago. Upon arriving in the city, she told them to wait at the depot, left, and never returned.

The Lakefront Depot, where young John Matthews and his sister twice jumped Chicago-bound trains
Library of Congress LC-D4-4806-A

The police contacted the children's frantic parents, who had not seen them since sending them off to Sunday school that morning. Their father, William Matthews, rushed down to Chicago to retrieve the children and sat with them as they recounted their fantastic story to a Milwaukee police detective. The children went on and on—about the "Chinaman and all sorts of funny people" they had seen in Chicago and the "cross" woman they had encountered at the Chicago police station, who was "saying horrid things because she did not like the bread they gave her to eat."

But their description of the kidnapping was evidently lacking, and both the police and the children's parents agreed that the pair had simply run away. Evidently, John had been punished by his mother for lying the day before and had determined to skip town. Police sent the kids home with their parents, who punished both for their flight to the south. But once again, little John Matthews felt that his penalty was undue. The very next day, he and Louisa once again walked to the Lakefront Depot, boarded a train, and—despite declarations that they did not like the city—disembarked in Chicago. There they once again claimed to have been kidnapped and were held at the police station to await their father.

Mr. Matthews had no idea how the children had managed to make the trip twice without paying and without drawing the suspicion of any adults aboard. He told the newspapers that his son was likely next bound for an industrial school.

"AM BEING KIDNAPPED..."
January 1939

A FTER COMPLETING his early afternoon run from Milwaukee to Chicago, a conductor for the Lake Shore Railroad found that a leather satchel had been left behind on his train. Inside was more than two thousand four hundred dollars in certified checks and a note that read, "Am being kidnapped for information. Call Milwaukee and Chicago police at once. Call the bank and let my parents know what happened. LeRoy Prodoehl."

Prodoehl was an eighteen-year-old messenger for Marshall and Ilsley Bank in Milwaukee. He had been reported missing about noon when he failed to return from his morning pick-ups. That evening, he appeared at the central police station in Chicago. He told police he had been abducted in Milwaukee by two men, forced onto a train, and drilled about information as to certified letter delivery at the bank. The pair was joined by another man in Chicago, where the men held him captive for nine hours, making a tour of north-side taverns and forcing the young man to buy them drinks. After the binge, they dumped him on a street corner just off the Loop, terrified but unharmed.

After five hours of questioning by Chicago police and agents of the FBI, Prodoehl confessed he had invented the entire story. He admitted there was but one perpetrator, a man in Milwaukee who had robbed him of twenty dollars and fled. Prodoehl was so scared about what his employers might do about the loss that he conjured up the kidnapping and fled the city.

But when the police in Milwaukee went over his receipts, he was found to be missing only $5.50. His story falling apart yet again, Prodoehl came clean one last time. He had stolen the money himself to pay off a debt. His bosses at the bank, more forgiving than one might expect, agreed to forget the incident and let him keep his job.

THE BABY PROBLEM
December 1931

M RS. AUGUST SEMROU of El Dorado, Wisconsin, was on her way to Milwaukee to see relatives. As she was waiting aboard the train at the West Bend depot on a layover, a panicked woman emerged from the crowd, thrust a newborn baby into her arms, and vanished. Moments later, the train departed, and the stunned Mrs. Semrou carried the babe all the way to Milwaukee, where she reported the incident to police. Authorities mulled over the tale for several days before confronting Mrs. Semrou. Asking her about some of the inconsistencies in her account, she admitted she had made it all up. Her friend had given birth to the child a few weeks earlier. Unable to keep the baby for reasons never disclosed publically, Mrs. Semrou had agreed to take it and raise it as her own. All she needed was a good cover story for how she had acquired the child. As the *Milwaukee Sentinel* noted, "[The story] seemed quite as good as another."

WOMAN WITH A CUT THROAT
March 1919

J UST A few minutes after entering Milwaukee on a train bound for the Union Depot in Walker's Point, a woman pulled open the collar of her blouse and ran a knife across her throat, opening a long and bloody wound that quickly rendered her unconscious. No one saw the woman, who was traveling alone, perform the deed. She was not found until the engine had come to a stop, one blood-covered hand at her collar, the other still clutching her weapon. After she was hurried to a hospital, no identification was found on her person. A letter in her pocket was addressed to an Appolonia Walters of Burlington, Wisconsin, and a tag on her luggage listed a train depot in the same city.

A conductor who was with the train in Chicago remembered talking with the woman, who said she had family in that city but that they wanted nothing to do with her. Police came to question her after her condition had stabilized, but she would only say that she was from Wellington, Wisconsin—a place the police soon discovered did not exist. Police suspected she was the Appolonia Walters to whom the letter was addressed, but the woman refused to give her name, age, or any motivation for the attempt on her life. Police put out a call for family members to come forward to help the troubled young woman, but could find none. The last news items mentioned about the woman indicated she would fully recover from her injuries.

THE HERMIT SUICIDES
July 1879

JOHN "BLACK Jack" MCDONALD was tramping through the Menomonee Valley on a hot summer morning, hoping to find an open job posting at the Milwaukee Road rail yards. Along the banks of the river, he found an old couple sitting in the shade of a weeping willow tree. He called out to them, asking for directions to a shop where he had once worked. The man answered back in German. McDonald, who did not speak German, continued on.

A short time later, unable to find the shop he was searching for, McDonald came back through the same part of the valley. He saw the same couple, this time standing just at the edge of the river, which had swollen due to recent storms. They held each other at their sides, hands clasped and cheek to cheek. The man was dressed in a brown cardigan coat, a black-and-white-striped vest, gray slacks, and a pair of beaten work boots. The woman wore a brown calico dress and tattered stockings. A blue-and-white scarf hung about her neck.

As McDonald walked closer, the couple began to wade into the water. At first, McDonald thought they might be trying to cross at a shallow point in the river. But as they trudged on, the waters grew higher. Finally, the pair toppled over, the woman submerging first, then the man. "What are you doing?" McDonald shouted out to them. "You are drowning each other!" McDonald could not swim. He called for help and ran to a nearby road but could find no one. He cut a pair of switches from a sapling and ran to the shore, hoping to reach out far enough that the couple could be pulled to safety, but there was no movement from the spot where they had sunk. After it became apparent the man and woman were lost to the waters, McDonald dashed off to the nearest police station.

Black Jack McDonald was well known to police. Upon first explaining what he had seen, there was some reluctance about believing the tale. But after assuring officers what he told them was no drunken tale, they followed him out to the valley, where they found the closely spaced footprints of the couple leading to their watery demise. Pulling the couple from the river—they remained clutched in each other's arms—police found no identification on either body. After two days, and no reports of any missing persons, the couple was buried in the cemetery at the city poor farm.

The next week, an old German couple appeared at a south-side police station and told police that the victims of what the papers had been calling the "hermit suicides" were a miserly old Bavarian couple who had lived for years in a little shack not far from where the drowning had occurred. A butcher known by the Germans had made regular meat deliveries to the Bavarians but had not heard from the old couple in two weeks.

A scene along the Menomonee River, where the unidentified couple drowned themselves

Historic Photo Collection / Milwaukee Public Library

The Germans had lived with the couple for a time and reported that the woman was insane, suspecting she had been pushed over the edge by the recent heat wave. They said the drowned couple's name was Sax but gave no other information. The Germans refused to give their own name or address, but promised police they would return the next day to provide more information. Police suspected the dead woman was the sister of the woman who came to the station that day, based on a physical resemblance. The couple never returned, and the identities of the pair pulled from the river were never confirmed.

ON THE FRINGE
July 1854

L ATE ONE evening, the telltale orange glow of a fire run beyond control was spotted at the very northern fringes of the
city. This desolate area, most likely between present-day Brady
Street and the Milwaukee River, was far from the nearest fire
company. The alarm bell sounded at 10:30, but none of the re-
sponding engines were able to find the blaze. Assuming the fire
was beyond the city boundary lines, the men returned home
and the matter was forgotten. But the next morning, a horrifying discovery was made among the scattered Polish settlements
that had formed in the area. The shanty home of Mathias Michaelovsky had burned to the ground. Found inside were five
charred bodies and two more poor souls so badly burned they
would not recover.

The shanty was a mere twelve feet by twelve feet, but at
the time of the fire had been home to at least ten people. In
addition to Michaelovsky, his wife, and their three children,
Johann Stoick also lived in the shack with his wife and three
daughters. Of the ten, just Michaelovsky, his wife, and one of
the Stoick daughters would survive. The scattered limbs of the
departed were found in a sickening state of disarray, entangled
with each other and spread about the room in a way that suggested a panicked attempt to flee the inferno. Authorities determined that the fire had started near the shanty's only exit,
near the stove, and had blocked any possible escape.

While nothing of the sort was reported in any other newspaper, and no further information on the claim was printed,
the *Milwaukee Sentinel* followed their initial reports on the fire
with a set of sensational claims. The paper wrote that evidence
was "unfold[ing] a shocking tale of prostitution, crime, and horrible death." The Michaelovsky shack, they said, was the regular site of drunkenness and immoral sexual acts. Unnamed
evidence, they claimed, pointed to a neighbor girl jealous of a
Michaelovsky daughter as the source of the fire. The culprit

was said to have already fled town on a steamer, her destination unknown.

BAD MAN

February 1929

"I SAW your picture in the newspaper," the letter read. "I know you and I just would like to take you out some night on a ride.... Shame on you. Don't try to find out who I am because I got you all doped out." This was the latest in a series of threatening letters mailed to Milwaukee girls in the early months of 1929. One of the recipients of these letters was Pearl Grove, a pretty seventeen-year-old student at Riverside High School. Police had no clues as to the origins of the letters but thought them to be the work of a recently immigrated male. Despite the note's brooding tone, Grove was adamant in not allowing the threat to interfere with her full academic schedule. But police insisted on putting the girl under constant supervision when outside of her North Avenue home.

The most chilling part of the letter claimed that Grove would be "bump[ed] off like Lillian Graef," a Milwaukee teen who had been brutally murdered and thrown from a secluded highway bridge just fifteen months before. The writer warned Grove that Lillian's awful fate is "what you will get some of these days." Police discounted the threat of danger but took no chances. They felt the writer was most likely mentally unwell and "satisfied in the fear he instills in the girls and their parents."

The note was signed, "Ed the Bad Man."

BLIND DATE

October 1927

A FORD coupe pulled up outside the Graef house at 82 East Garfield Avenue. Inside the home, nineteen-year-old Lillian Graef, the youngest of the family's seven children, grabbed her coat and pulled a pink hat over her ears. She had never met the man in the coupe. The date had been set up by Lillian's sister Mildred. Even Mildred had met the man—known only as Jack—just once. A few days prior, waiting at a street car stop at Murray and North Avenues, Jack pulled up in his jaunty Ford and offered the girl a ride. After taking Mildred to her Brady Street destination, Jack asked for her name and phone number. Mildred had a steady, but Jack was handsome and gentleman-ly, so she gave him her sister's name instead. A few days later, their date was set. "I wonder what this goof looks like," Lillian remarked to Mildred just before she left the house.

Mildred watched her sister bound down the front walk, to-ward Jack and the coupe. "Jack got out of the car and opened the door for her and said something I couldn't hear. Lillian said, 'Oh, that's all right,'" Mildred later told police. "Then, they drove away." It was the last time she ever saw her sister alive.

Lillian Graef possessed tomboyish good looks—slender and moonfaced with a wide smile and a moppish brown bob. But only recently had she started going on dates. She was consid-ered by her friends and classmates to be something of a home-body, quiet and studious, and preferring books to boys. When she did go out, she expected her companions to be very well mannered. Boys from her school told of slapped faces following pecks on her cheek. Girls spoke of her "aversion" to things like necking and petting.

Lillian worked as a clerk at the Ramhorst Candy Store at 812 North Third Street. She had worked on the day she vanished, even begging off early so she would have time to get ready and eat dinner before Jack picked her up. During that last shift, a man called on Lillian at the candy shop. He was a regular pa-tron of the place, visiting nearly every Tuesday and Thursday that Lillian worked for several months. No one knew his name, but his paunchy shape and bald head had become very familiar.

He was somewhere between forty and fifty, dressed pricey and sharp, and drove a dark Cadillac. Most assumed him to be a wealthy admirer of the young girl. Lillian never spoke about the man to her friends but at least once had been heard to say, "There goes Daddy," when a dark Cadillac passed by.

Three weeks after she left on her blind date, Lillian's battered body was found in the Fox River, snagged on a log beneath the newly constructed Highway 19 bridge about three miles north of Waukesha. She had been struck in the head at least eleven times with a semisharp instrument and strangled with her own scarf. Shattered digits on both hands and a dent in her school ring indicated she had attempted to fight off her attacker. Lillian was already dead when her body was dropped into the water from an old steel bridge on a seldom-used side road, a few hundred yards upriver from where it was recovered. A recent rainstorm had swollen the stream and dislodged the body. Authorities doubted the crime was of a sexual nature, as she was still fully dressed and her body showed no signs of assault. The time of her death was approximated at one hour after she was picked up by Jack, indicating that she was either killed somewhere within the city limits and then taken to the bridge, or taken there directly and murdered at the scene. The only items missing from her body were a decorative breast pin and her pink hat.

Although it had been nearly a month since Lillian's disappearance, detectives had only considered the case a potential homicide for about ten days. Their initial suspicion was that she had eloped with Jack and was afraid to return home. And it was not until the body was recovered that they finally issued a widespread alert for her mysterious date. Jack was described by Mildred as being in his mid- to late twenties, dark-haired, slender, and well spoken. He had mentioned his last name during their brief encounter in his coupe, but she could not recall what it was. Initially, police suspected that Jack might have been a victim of the same attacker who killed Lillian—the sad end to an unprovoked assault on a young, joy-riding couple. But no reported missing persons matched his description. At first sought only for questioning, Jack was the prime suspect in the crime within days of the discovery of the body. Also sought was the older man now known as "Cadillac Daddy." Despite months of regular calls at the Ramhorst shop, he was never seen again after Lillian's disappearance.

In the days after Lillian was pulled from the river, hundreds of curious locals drove out to the Highway 19 bridge to search for clues. Several pink hats, found in all corners of the county, were brought to authorities on the hopes they could help catch the killer. As Lillian was laid to rest in a closed-casket ceremony—not even her family was allowed to see the mangled corpse—police fanned out across the city to question every man who had been accused of a sex crime in recent years as to his whereabouts on the night of the murder. Plainclothes officers also began mingling with the crowds near the Fox River, hoping to catch the killer having returned to the scene.

Meanwhile, scores of tips on Jack and Cadillac Daddy poured in from the public. Detectives were ordered down to Chicago to search for a "dressy" man who drove a Cadillac and was rumored to have "admired" a young Milwaukee girl. Police also investigated allegations that a young Milwaukee man sold his Ford coupe for a fraction of its worth on the day Lillian's body was found. Rumors abounded that the killing was the work of Chicagoland gangsters who had been involved in the bootlegging business with the Graef family. A grudge between the two, it was gossiped, led to a carload of men following Jack and Lillian into the country that night and rubbing the girl out as retaliation.

That night after Lillian's funeral, a Mount Horeb couple was attacked along Highway 18 near Dousman. Alvin Greenwald was badly beaten and left for dead. His wife, Emma, was brutally raped and murdered. In the days that followed, newspapers grimly connected the two attacks. A long list of similar unsolved killings was printed by the *Milwaukee Senti-nel*—Madelynne Latimer and Jimmy Sears, a handsome young couple found shot to death in a ditch near Kenosha in 1925; Jackson Carlisle, a "soldier of fortune and adventurer" found murdered in the same area the following year; Walter Frentz, a Racine boy who was found drowned south of West Allis; and Julia Twardowski, a south-side Milwaukee girl found dead at the county line just a few months before Lillian's death. The paper wrote of "shooting fools" who prowled the back roads in the evenings, shooting at cars and homes, and just maybe hunting young couples.

Despite the worries of a repeat killer on the loose, the Green-wald case proved to have no connection to the Graef killing. Within days of the attack, Alvin Greenwald confessed to hiring a man to slay his wife in an attempt to collect on her life insurance policy. But while the book was closed on that killing, police were groping in the dark for Jack and Cadillac Daddy. In early December, twenty thousand flyers with an artist's sketch of Cadillac Daddy were sent all over the county but brought no useful tips. In late January 1928, two St. Paul women came forward to say that Jack was a friend of the man hired to kill Emma Greenwald and that he was currently working as a cab driver in Chicago. Nothing came of the claim.

The next month, every man in Milwaukee who owned or had access to a Ford coupe on the evening of Lillian's murder was ordered to report to the central station to be viewed by Mildred Graef. For several weeks, she went to the station every night, viewing hundreds of men and clearing them all. Each man, after posing for Mildred, was given a card declaring that he was no longer considered a suspect in the matter. As late as 1931, Mildred was still being called in to view men police suspected of being the man who took Lillian on her final ride. To each one, she forlornly shook her head. Neither Jack nor Cadillac Daddy were ever positively identified and the murder of Lillian Graef remains unsolved.

THE WOMAN AT THE BREAKWATER
June 1898

A ROUND A quarter past eight on a mild summer evening, a well-dressed man rented a sixteen-foot rowboat from a stand at the lakefront foot of Mason Street, just to the north of the Chicago and North Western Railroad depot. He wore a stiff, black hat and carried a heavy satchel. He was accompanied by a lovely young woman, about thirty years of age, dressed in a dark skirt and light-colored shirtwaist. Shortly after the pair paddled off into the blackening night, an eastern wind turned the lake waters choppy.

After about three hours, the boys tending the stand began to think that the couple had encountered trouble. With the now-total darkness and increasingly disagreeable seas, they thought the couple might have been unable to find the landing and ditched the boat somewhere along the beach. Just as the boys were preparing to head out in search of the vessel, it appeared from the darkness. The man was alone. "Where is your lady friend?" one of the boys asked.

"I left her at Lake Park," the man said. "The water became choppy and she was afraid to return." The boys remarked that rowing to the landing at the park and back in three hours was a substantial feat. The round-trip journey was nearly seven miles. The man said he had lived a difficult life and was used to hard work. He even remarked that he was about to leave the area for the Canadian Yukon, which was in the midst of a gold rush. The man paid the rental fee in silver coins and left, his satchel appearing much lighter than it had been before.

About six weeks later, a body washed up at the government pier off North Point. It was an adult woman, dressed only in undergarments, stockings, and shoes. A chain was wrapped snugly around her waist, looped twice and shackled to a twenty-five-pound horse-hitching weight. Police noted the woman had very slender and delicate hands and feet, and probably "occupied a comparatively high station in life." Only a few minutes after being removed from the water, the body collapsed into a "shapeless mass." It was quickly estimated that the woman had been killed on a vessel, stripped, and thrown in the water. Unable to reconstruct what the young woman might have looked like, police instead focused on the physical clues found with the body. The daily newspapers carried images of the hitching weight, and the tattered underthings taken from the body were kept on public display at the central station.

A young woman dives from a rowboat similar to the one that carried an unknown woman to her fate.
WHi Image ID 60306

The day after the body was recovered, the boat stand boys came forward with their story. Investigators found the unknown man's story of dropping his date at Lake Park highly unlikely, as the landing there was difficult to maneuver and more than a mile from the nearest street car stop. No woman, it was thought, would have asked to be left there alone and at night, no matter how frightened she was of the lake roll. As police looked into the boys' story, the crew of the tugboat *Hagerman* reported they had seen a similar couple in a rowboat about

9:30 that same evening, far from the shore and not headed in the direction of the park. A few days later, a teamster reported that a weight of his identical to the one recovered had been stolen from him the day before the couple rented the boat. It was taken from the park near the flushing tunnel on the lakefront, just miles from the boat rental stand.

But if the police had a general idea as to how the crime was committed, they still had no clue as to the identities of those involved. Hundreds of Milwaukeeans were drawn to the display of the garments, including "curious ones," who were, in the words of the *Milwaukee Sentinel*, "impelled by a morbid interest in gruesome things [and] inspected the discolored garments with an evident pleasure." Scores of tips revealed dozens of women, either Milwaukee residents or visitors, who could not be located by loved ones. One woman feared the departed to be her daughter, whom she had not heard from in some time and was quite unhappily married to a man who had threatened on several occasions to kill her. Another tip told of a woman who had taken up with a married man. When the situation turned sour, the man told a friend of the woman that he gave her some money and she left town. The missing woman's friend suspected he was not telling the truth. One man told police his wife had run off on him and was last known to be living in Milwaukee. He asked for, and was given, a piece of lace from the underclothes found on the body. He refused to give his name but promised to return the next day with more information. He was never seen again. A Chicago man made the trip north and said the clothes looked very similar to those owned by his wife, who had walked out on him some time ago. Examining the teeth from the corpse, however, he became convinced the body was not that of his wife. He was fairly unmoved during the process, telling police he was merely curious as to the identity of the body and did not care one whit if his wife was alive or dead.

Despite the case's publicity, no positive identification of the body was ever made. Three days after the woman at the breakwater was recovered, she was buried in the potter's field at the county poor farm, along the south bank of Menomonee River to the west of the city, to be forever eulogized as "Name Unknown."

BLOOD MONEY
August 1910

IT WAS just past 6:00 a.m. when someone found an unlocked door and slipped into the basement of the boardinghouse at 281 Jackson Street in Milwaukee's Third Ward. About fifty people lived in the three-story building, the majority of them Italian laborers. Most residents of the place had already set out for work that morning, leaving it mostly empty as a violent summer storm laid sheets of rain on the neighborhood and rattled its windows with vicious thunderclaps. Twenty-three-year-old Italian immigrant Antonio Navetta was one of the handful who remained in the house. Navetta was sick and bedbound for the day. His illness had come on the heels of a major injury sustained while working for the Gillen Construction Company on the city's government pier. An emergency operation was needed to save his life, and his injuries left Navetta despondent for weeks.

An insurance settlement on the incident paid Navetta five hundred dollars, which he had withdrawn from the bank in cash the day before the unknown person entered the basement of his boardinghouse. As the intruder crept through the maze of basement rooms toward Navetta's bedroom, a letter from Navetta's sweetheart back in Italy sat in a bundle at the post office. It brought news that she would soon be bound for Milwaukee. Navetta planned to use the five hundred dollars for their wedding.

Police speculated that the intruder did not expect to find anyone at home. Coming across Navetta in bed, he attempted to gag the man but woke him in the process. Navetta had been weakened by his illness but had enough fight in him to ignite a violent struggle. The battle between the two upended the cot on which he had been sleeping and snapped the leg of a nearby table. As Navetta grappled with the intruder, two women were at home and awake one floor above, but the sounds of the struggle were masked by the whir of their sewing machines and the steady noise of the storm. Unable to subdue Navetta, the intruder pulled a knife and ran its six-inch blade into the Italian's throat, drew it back, and slashed again, striking with such a fury that the blade went through Navetta's neck and nicked one of his vertebrae. The blows cut both his jugular vein and his carotid artery, spewing forth a horrible tide of blood as Navetta crumpled to the floor.

Third Ward boardinghouses similar to the one in which Antonio Navetta lived
Library of Congress LC-USF34-006043-D

As Navetta clamped a hand to his neck in a futile attempt to save himself, the intruder tore through the little apartment, sacking the place in search of the roll of bills Navetta had taken from the bank. There was so much blood on his hands that his movements left specks of red on the walls of the rooms as he searched for the cash. He finally found it stashed in a trunk and, after wiping his hands on a towel and placing it back on its hook, left the house through the front door.

The storm cut the workday short for Navetta's six room-mates, who began to return to the boardinghouse about 9:30 a.m. They found Navetta dead and their home disrupted "in the wildest confusion." The blood had pooled so thickly on the floor that one of his roommates, suspecting that Navetta had slit his own throat, used a file to search the red puddle for a blade. Quickly, the police were summoned and made a search of the scene. The killer left no clues behind and no witnesses reported seeing anyone in the area. Police denied that the killing was related to the long-whispered presence of organized crime in the Third Ward.

The day after Navetta's murder, blood-soaked bills began to turn up in various locations in the neighborhood. The first was taken by a bartender at an unnamed Italian saloon. The five-dollar bill, half-stained red, was used to buy a quart of whiskey. The men did not notice the stain until after the customer had left and could provide no details about his appearance. In the following days a ten-dollar bill in a similar state was deposited at a Third Ward bank and another red-tinged five landed at a butcher shop. No leads came from any of the blood-stained cash.

Despite their insistence that there was no mafia connection to the crime, the police received tips that led them to bring in Vito Guardalebene, the neighborhood's undisputed don, and other prominent men of business with alleged "connections" for questioning. "We are working on a big thing," said Otto Riemer, the police inspector who interrogated Guardalebene told the press. "If what we believe from the evidence presented to us is true then this is something bigger than has engaged our attention for a long time."

But Riemer's predictions of a "big thing" fizzled. Those who talked did not know, and those who knew never talked. No arrests were ever made in the case and what the *Milwaukee Sentinel* called "one of the most brutal crimes ever committed in this city" remains unsolved.

BLACK HAND
June 1912

D ARKNESS STILL covered the Third Ward when Dominic Leone left his home at 146 Detroit Street[1] for his job as superintendent at the city garbage plant near the straight cut that connected Lake Michigan with Milwaukee's rivers. The twenty-eight-year-old Leone had immigrated to the United States from Italy in 1902. He had been in Milwaukee since 1905 and worked as a laborer. He became active in politics and was such an active and gifted campaigner that he soon collected on the spoils of his work. After helping the city's nonpartisan slate win big in the 1912 municipal elections, he was appointed to his post at the garbage plant. But his work had also earned him a dedicated team of enemies. Still, as he strode to work that morning, he was regarded as one of the leading citizens of the Third Ward's "Italian colony": honest, well liked, and kind.

It was about 3:20 a.m. when Leone passed underneath a gaslight on Jefferson Street, splashing him with light just long enough for the man hidden in the alleyway to step out and fire his single-barreled shotgun into Leone's chest. The report of the gun cracked the silent air of the summer morning and woke neighbors for a block in every direction. Leone's wife, Anna, was one of the many jolted upright by the shot. She was immediately overtaken by fear for her husband's safety. Leone was hit in three places by the shot, later found to be of an old-fashioned, homemade variety. One shard pierced his shoulder while two more landed in his chest, one tearing into his heart. Leone cried out for help as he staggered into the road. A thin trail of blood followed him across the street to a bench in front of the Michael Cesaro saloon. A beat cop who had heard the shot found him there a few minutes later, sitting upright but departed from this world.

---

1. Now St. Paul Avenue

By the time the sun had risen, hundreds of Third Ward residents had joined the police in searching for clues, but none were uncovered. Although they searched side-by-side for Leone's killers, the Milwaukee Police Department and the denizens of the Italian Third Ward were hardly in cooperation. Of the five murders that had occurred in the neighborhood over the previous six years, none had been solved. In the Third Ward, it was the neighborhood's obligation to see that justice was carried out. If there was information that could aid the course of such justice, it was not shared with the police.

"The death of Leone will be avenged and other deaths will probably follow," a Milwaukee detective told the *Milwaukee Journal* the day Leone was killed. "Leone often told me before his death that he could probably place his hands on the men guilty of the murders in the Italian colony over the past two years but admitted that he was afraid to try it. The moment one Italian 'squealed,' he said, his death warrant was signed, and this was so well understood that we have never been able to obtain even the slightest information." Even on their deathbeds, the papers reported, maimed and dying Italians would not name those who harmed them.

So eager was the police department to upset this trend that police chief John Janssen arrived on the scene to personally aid in the investigation and interviewing of witnesses. But it was of little use. By the next day, the *Milwaukee Sentinel* reported that police had pulled back in their investigation and were "awaiting the action of friends of the young Italian leader" who had "begun to search throughout the United States for the assailant in the underground channels of Italian societies which work silently and secretly."

The only minor break the police got in the case was when an officer overheard a group of children taunting an old man who peddled fruit in the neighborhood. "Your uncle killed Leone! Your uncle killed Leone!" they were heard calling at him the day of the murder. Police hauled in the man and the children involved, all of whom denied any knowledge of the crime. The

kids not only denied knowing anything about Leone or his killer but said they had never shouted anything at the man. "There
is no question the children were shouting those words," Captain John Sullivan told the *Journal*. "They evidently overheard
some talk by their parents but they knew enough to keep quiet."

Three days after his murder, a funeral service was held for
Leone at the Madonna di Pompeii Church on Jackson Street.
Leone's cousin, Father Domenic Leone, presided over the service. Father Leone was one of the few locals who cooperated with
the police. "I do not know whether these men were guilty or not
but I suspected them and told the police," he later said. "No evidence could be gotten, but they know I accused them." Fears of
a retaliatory attack, either on those suspected in Leone's death
or those thought to be fingering the killers, led police to station "scores" of officers among the mourners as they marched
from the church to Cavalry Cemetery on Blue Mound Road.

As the somber procession headed west, a detective found the
murder weapon stashed under a trash pile in the rear lot of a
Milwaukee Street home, about a half block from the scene of the
crime. The discovery of the gun yielded little in the way of the
police catching whoever had wielded it. Whispers were heard
that Leone was done away by men he refused to hire at the garbage plant. Others gossiped that he had been killed for refusing to pay tribute to local "Black Hand" leaders. Anna Leone,
however, was too bereft for such talk. "I don't know about these
societies, these 'Black Hands,' or these murders. I never asked
about them for I loved my husband and was not afraid of his
nationality," she told the *Journal*. "He was always kind and
considerate, never rough and ill-mannered like the others. Although he was Italian and I am German, my mother did not
object to our marriage when she saw what a gentleman he was."

In the month that followed the murder of Leone, several city
trash cart drivers who shared Leone's political sympathies resigned their jobs over fears that the forces who did away with
their boss might not have completed their purge. Police spoke
of two rival factions struggling for control of the area and the

patronage jobs centered there. Blood was spilled, but mouths remained shut. The identities of those who ended the life of Dominic Leone, and the price they paid for that crime, are secrets the Third Ward never shared.

THE MISSING HEAD
December 1890

"HELLO, WHAT'S this?" the *Milwaukee Sentinel* reported a workman to have said as his shovel struck a wooden box. "A coffin, sure enough!" The man was part of the team excavating a portion of the eastern bank of the Milwaukee River, working to construct the brand-new bridge at Michigan Street. About five feet beneath ground level, a narrow wooden box was uncovered. As the men dug around the box, its edges crumbled and its lid fell apart, revealing a nearly intact skeleton of an adult male. The men gently removed the bones from the box and laid them out on the sidewalk. As they arranged them in their living shape, a light snow began to fall and dozens of passersby gathered to watch. After emptying the box, someone called out that their mystery skeleton was missing its skull.

No one was able to remember a time when bodies were buried in such a location. James Buck, pioneer historian of the city, said that the bones were unlikely to have belonged to a Native American but were most probably the remnants of a murdered French fur trader. The burial appeared to have been a hasty one, but a wooden slab found at the top end of the makeshift coffin suggested that the site, for a time, had been marked. A broken piece of iron was found near the coffin, which some suspected was the murder weapon. As for the missing head, Buck hypothesized it had been hacked off and tossed in the river to prevent the identification of the body. It was generally assumed that the man had died sometime in the 1830s. As darkness fell on the worksite, the bones were collected by the city coroner, who had them "reburied not quite so close to the river."

IN THE ATTIC
September 1858

W ORKING TO repair a building near West Water and Tam-
arack Streets,[1] a structure in a "usually quiet neighborhood," a workman clearing out the upper floors made a
horrifying discovery. Hidden beneath a pile of trash in a corner
of the attic was a startlingly well-persevered female skeleton.
The smooth, white bones had no trace of flesh remaining. The
only visible damage was a single fractured rib. The building
had been vacant for more than fifteen months and was most
recently occupied by a physician who had since left the city. The
Milwaukee Sentinel, reporting on the matter, observed that "in
these times...we doubt not that but similar 'skeletons' can be
found in every 'attic' in the city." No record survives of the bones
ever having been identified.

NOT JOHN DWYER
April 1855

S OME FISHERMEN happened upon a terrible sight while working near the mouth of the Milwaukee River. Surfacing after
an estimated three months in the water was a badly mutilated
male corpse, his legs hacked off, hands bound tight, and throat
cut. The body had been tied up in a cotton bag and then stuffed
into a coffee sack and cinched about the neck with a sailor's
knot—bound so skillfully that "no landsman could dream of
making it." The head of the victim displayed a horrific axe
wound that had split open the skull. It was impossible to determine by which trauma the man had died.

Horrific discoveries of this type had become a disturbingly
regular occurrence on Milwaukee's waterways. This was the

---

1. Now Plankinton and State Streets

third badly mangled body to be found in recent months. "The river and the lake," wrote the *Milwaukee Sentinel*, "are almost daily giving up the mangled bodies of men who have been deprived of life by foul violence."

The black-haired victim was laid out at the docks near the lakefront Checkered Warehouse so locals might be able to identify him. A mate from the vessel *Ole Bull* recognized the body as that of John Dwyer, a sailor who had worked in Milwaukee the previous winter. Others soon concurred, pointing to a scar on the battered face of the body that matched one worn by Dwyer. No one was found who could remember seeing Dwyer since Christmas. "No sane man," the *Sentinel* wrote, "could have doubted that the remains found were those of John Dwyer."

In tracking down former acquaintances of Dwyer to testify as to the body's identity, the police heard of a man named Harris, who was said to have worked with Dwyer. They found Harris laboring at a lakefront dock and, upon asking him about Dwyer, discovered the supposedly dead man to be very much alive. He was working at the same dock, within miles of where the body had been found. The police found Dwyer to be "ready to make an oath" that the torso in the river—which would remain unidentified—was not his.

"ORDER OF THE DAY"
July 1856

ONE SUMMER afternoon, a set of clothing was found beneath a pile of lumber at the shipyards along the Milwaukee River. The parcel consisted of a pair of dungaree overalls, a white linen shirt with the initials "G.B." on the pocket, and a red cotton handkerchief. The front of the shirt was stained with what appeared to be a considerable amount of blood. Six days later, a boy paddling a boat on the river discovered a man's head—viciously hacked from its body—afloat in the water. The

Milwaukee Sentinel, reporting on the discovery, admitted they had no idea where the item had come from, nor what became of it after the boy pulled it into his boat. "Inquests," the paper wrote, "are not the order of the day."

TELLING
May 1874

O N A spring Sunday afternoon, the bloated little body of three-year-old Joseph Dehm was found at the west end of the Oneida Street[1] bridge. The boy had wandered away from his Market Street home more than three weeks earlier and had been the subject of an intensive search that covered both the physical confines of the city and certain, less tangible realms of existence. Within days of the boy's disappearance, his parents sought the aid of a fortune-teller. At the time, it was said that Milwaukee was home to more seers, mediums, and palmists than any city of comparable size in the nation. The old woman the Dehms visited said their son had been kidnapped.

This theory was taken up as fact by the police, who claimed that the boy, after realizing he was lost a few blocks from home, was found crying by a man who said he would take the child to his mother. This man was last seen, the *Milwaukee Sentinel* reported, walking south along the Milwaukee River. But just as quickly as the kidnapping story was advanced, it was retracted. After "great trouble and expense" on the part of the Dehms and no clues to support the kidnapping theory or the story of the southbound man, the police said it was most likely that the boy had fallen in the river and drowned.

Within a few days of the discovery of Joseph Dehm, city authorities took under consideration a proposal to institute a one-hundred-dollar permit fee for all those wishing to tell fortunes in Milwaukee. The common council did the opponents of

---

1. Now Wells Street

claimed clairvoyancy one better, banning the practice outright within city limits. Those who continued openly in the trade were arrested while others, perhaps possessed of a knack for keeping one step ahead of the authorities, took their practices underground without ever arousing suspicion.

A fortune-teller plies her trade.
WHI Image ID 57661

HEART FAILURE
January 1880

THE UNNAMED young man worked at the downtown Aschermann and Company cigar factory. The unnamed young woman lived at home with her parents on North Third Street. As reported by the *Chicago Tribune* in an article titled "A Milwaukee Romance," they had met in some unremarkable way and he asked to call on her. She said that he could. In the company of family, the man and woman spent time together. He fell in love. She did not. He proposed marriage. She refused.

Then the young woman's parents interceded. They urged her to reconsider and she did. She agreed to marry him. But the engagement was an unhappy one. She had told him on prior occasions that she did not love him. But at his urging, and that of her parents, she gave the matter some time. Over the course of their engagement, however, it became plain to the young woman that she could never love this man. Finally, she admitted this to him, calling off the marriage and crushing the young man's hopes. He begged her to reconsider, to give it more time. He tried everything he could think of, but she refused to change her mind.

Finally—exhausted, broken, and frantic—he called the "curse of heaven" upon her head. He called on the spirit of his departed mother to visit the young woman in the dead of night. He commanded his mother to carry a burning candle and to be "clad in the garments of the grave." He swore his mother would appear beside her peaceful bed and jolt her from her slumber.

The woman, being very superstitious, took the curse with a deadly kind of seriousness. It kept her up nights as she feared the appearance of the apparition. Finally, having fretted over it so much, her mind began to fill the gaps her fear had created. Her jilted lover's dead mother began to appear, clad in rags and clutching a candle, acting on the anguished demands of her son. According to the *Tribune*, the vision "heaped mute imprecations upon her head." The stress of the "ghost" was too much for the frail young woman. She lapsed into a sickness and, despite the efforts of attending physicians, continued to worsen. Her former fiancé tried to visit her after she took ill, but upon entering her room the woman, too weakened to speak, waved him away. Despite the efforts of her attending physicians, the woman died within a few days of the dead mother's first appearance. Doctors listed "heart failure" as the official cause of death.

THE GIRL WHO COULDN'T MOVE
December 1898

O N AN unremarkable July morning, the mother of twenty-three-year-old Tony Broscheit came into the girl's bedroom to wake her for the day. Tony and her family lived in the basement apartment of a building near the corner of Marshall and Mason Streets. Her father was the building's janitor and she often helped him in his duties. Tony did not rouse at her mother's call that morning, so she was left to sleep. She had been working especially hard as of late, and Mrs. Broscheit felt the girl could use the extra rest. But when she returned later, she found her daughter in a disturbing state. She could still not be awoken, but her eyes were open wide, staring off at a corner of the little room. She responded to neither sound nor touch and made no movements beside her shallow breaths and the blinking of her eyes.

Through the summer and into the fall, the remarkable case of Tony Broscheit baffled doctors all over the city. She sometimes shifted her eyes about the room, sometimes scanning the faces of the many men who attempted to cure her of her condition, but her eyes remained mostly fixated on the corner of the room. On very rare occasions, her lips made a feeble attempt at a smile or parted ever so slightly as if in an attempt to speak. She seemed trapped in a state that was not sleep nor waking life.

Some doctors hypothesized that her condition was brought on by overwork, but she was known to have fallen into a similar state once before in her teens, although for a much shorter period of time. As winter came, the strain of Tony's sickness became too much for her family to bear. A near-constant medical watch was kept on the girl, who needed regular feedings by forcing food between her rigidly clenched teeth. The family decided that if she did not recover by Christmas, she would be sent to the asylum at Wauwatosa.

On December 20, doctors J. W. Cutler and M. G. Violet examined the girl and told her parents that the condition was the
result of self-hypnosis brought on by hysteria. The girl was so
agitated that she had simply shut herself down. Newspapers reported that for several days, the doctors administered their own
hypnosis to Tony, demanding her to obey them through a series
of "suggestive therapeutics." On December 24, it was reported,
Tony responded to stimuli for the first time since July, "furnishing evidence that her mind, as well as her body, belong in
this world." By Christmas Day, she had sat up and was speaking with friends, and doctors expected her to fully recover.

THE FLYING MACHINE
December 1896

L ATE ONE afternoon, Herman Nunnemacher, a Milwaukeean of considerable wealth and notoriety, happened to look
east from the window of the Pfister Hotel suite in which he
lived. Above the bay, high in the air and moving against the
winds, he saw something he could not identify. Nunnemacher
grabbed a nearby pair of field glasses and took aim on the object. It appeared to be a flying machine piloted by small figures
working its wings. Nunnemacher grabbed his coat and hat and
ran downstairs and into the street for a better look, but by then,
the vessel had vanished. Resigned that the object had passed
over the city "on its way to the North Pole," he went back to his
room. But, within ten minutes' time, the object had reappeared
over the lake. This time, Nunnemacher made no secret of his
sighting and ran into the hotel lobby. "It is there again," he
shouted. "A flying machine!"

Hundreds of others reported seeing the same object, "positive," the *Chicago Tribune* reported, "that it was a sure-enough
flying machine." Men along the lakefront, however, reported
seeing something quite different. They claimed to have witnessed two unknown men flying a large, tailless kite with long

wings. The object was flown with a heavy, metal wire that the men used to send "a number of signals" to the device. The paper claimed the US Army had been dabbling with similar contraptions for months.

THE OLD JARVIS HOUSE
June 1898

IT WAS requested of the commissioner of public works, Paul Muenzberg, that a vacant home at the corner of Grand Avenue and Twenty-second Street, in the heart of one of Milwaukee's most fashionable districts, be demolished by the city. The house, petitioners claimed, was haunted.

For many years, the house had been occupied by the Jarvis sisters. But when they left the city for the East Coast in the late 1880s, the structure fell into disrepair. At first it became a hangout for local boys, who used it as a clubhouse and made work of its windows with well-aimed stones. A habit of these boys—done to frighten passersby—was to stage evening "apparitions" in the windows using candlelight and shadows. Eventually tramps and drifters took control of the property and boarded over the windows to secure it against the elements and anyone who might wish to chase them from what had become a rent-free Grand Avenue flophouse.

The strange and covert goings-on at the place only heightened its reputation as a haunted house. Just across the street from the Grand Avenue Congregational Church and within shouting distance of the Pabst Mansion, the property sat against the south end of the city's first Catholic cemetery. The old cemetery was abandoned in the late 1850s with most—but not all—of its bodies removed. This fact, according to newspaper reports, "gave a sacredness to the manifestations of the boys." Parents used the legends of displaced corpses and the old pranks played at the house to scare their own children from the property. By the late 1890s, "even older persons trembled before [the house's] terrible presence." One west-side social club held initiation meetings at the house and made a night's sleep in the place a prerequisite for membership.

Muenzberg refused to act on the complaint, saying there were no grounds for condemning the structure. A city attorney also expressed doubt that the common council had any power in the matter, as there were no municipal ordinances designed to deal with annoyances by the undead.

THE HOUSE ON THE RAVINE

August 1875

L EGENDS ABOUT the old house near the river were well known in Milwaukee. The place sat along a bluff to the west of the Milwaukee River, planted on a road between the reservoir and an old ravine in which, the *Milwaukee Sentinel* asserted, "many a desperate deed was done in the early days of the settlement." The house was said to be the target of the cannon used by Solomon Juneau's east-side village to threaten Byron Kilbourn's westsiders during the "Bridge War" of 1845, a structure that might have been leveled if the two sides had not come to an amicable settlement and unified as a city. But as Milwaukee entered its fourth decade, the place was best known as the most notoriously haunted place in town.

One late-summer afternoon, the *Sentinel* sent a man to investigate the house and its alleged other-worldly inhabitants. He found the home's owner, an old German man, next door. The German gladly showed him around. A Polish family left the place early that summer, and it had been vacant since. They left quickly, departing as most former tenants did with stories of odd happenings. The property owner himself was aware of the stories and could even contribute his own. One night shortly after the Polish family left, he told the reporter, he observed a window in one of the house's lower rooms glowing brightly. Thinking the place was on fire, he rushed to the building, but no sooner had he made it to the front door than the light was gone. Still curious, he was about to go inside, but upon turning the key, the light returned with a startling brilliance. Henceforth, this became a regular occurrence at the place, the man claimed, with lights burning several evenings in a row, before going dark again for weeks.

The house itself was in a sickly state. It was a plain, two-story clapboard structure, grayed and weather-beaten on its exterior and "dark, dingy, and dismal within." The owner recalled that some time back, a pair of Englishmen curious about the place had asked him if they could spend an evening there just to see what all the talk was about. The German obliged them, handing them the key and even a pair of blankets. When he went to check on the men the following morning, he found the front door wide open and the blankets left rumpled on the floor. But the men were nowhere to be found.

The German remembered their names, however, and the *Sentinel* man tracked one of them, George Heath, to the Menomonee Valley railroad yard where he worked. Heath and his friend, Henry Jordan, had stayed at the place on a lark. Heath claimed he never believed in ghosts and, after securing the key and looking about the old place, even had a good laugh with Jordan about the old spook stories. It seemed silly, he said, to be so worried over a place "as still as the grave." After their chuckle, the pair went for a walk and had a smoke, then returned for bed. Their slumber, however, was fleeting. Heath said that not long after retiring, the sound of rapid footsteps jolted them awake. On the floor above, they heard what sounded to be jumping, and then a scuffle. After a panic-torn shriek, they heard a heavy thud, not at all dissimilar, Heath said, to a lifeless body falling to the floor. Then there was silence. Jordan slowly climbed the stairs and was about to strike a match when an upper room in the house began to glow brightly. The two men found nothing in the illuminated room and soon returned to their blankets. When, some fifteen minutes later, the entire scenario replayed itself, the pair made haste for their homes, leaving behind another chapter in the whispered history of the Haunted House of Kilbourntown. The reporter noted that Heath was known as a reliable and upstanding citizen but conveyed the story with a certain skepticism. When the story was published, it led with a headline that read IT MAY BE RATS.

INCENDIARY
November 1893

O N A still autumn evening, Frank Zieman's Center Street feed store went up in a terrific blaze. As fire companies rushed to the scene, Zieman and his neighbors gathered around the place, watching the horrible flames take their toll. One of the men in the crowd, a twenty-six-year-old German laborer named Henry Falk, approached Zieman and made a peculiar comment. Falk told Zieman in an almost apologetic tone that he had no hard feelings against him. He refused to elaborate on his statement and quickly left the scene. Soon after his hasty departure, the Ritzke Saloon, just blocks from the feed store, also caught fire. Later still, the barn of John Just on Holton Street went up in a burst of flames, leveling the structure and killing two horses.

Based on Zieman's tip about his "confession" on Center Street, police arrested Falk on suspicion of arson. He eventually confessed to setting the Zieman and Ritzke fires but denied firing the Just barn. He also admitted that he had set three fires at the mill of the C.A. Beck Company, where he had previously worked. After the first two fires at the mill, the company placed a hired man on the grounds in hopes of catching the perpetrator. Falk waited two weeks before the man was finally pulled from his detail. The first night the grounds were unwatched, Falk set a massive blaze that caused ten thousand dollars in damages.

Police suspected Falk of many other unexplained fires in the city over the previous year, but the man denied any other incendiary activity. Falk said he had no grievance with any of the people whose property he attacked. He said the urge to set fires came over him when he was drinking. He could not explain his compulsion.

CRAZY FRITZ
December 1928

A SHOCKING note was received at the Lederer farm in Grafton one afternoon. It read, "I am Fritz Lederer; they did not bury me, and I want to see my mother again." Frederick "Fritz" Lederer had drowned in the Chippewa River at age seventeen, some twenty years earlier—or so his family had always believed.

John Lederer, Fritz's brother, sent a relative to the Milwaukee address the note had given. The relative took the man living at the address, described as a sandy-haired, "mad-eyed" wanderer, to a nearby police station. There, between fits of sobbing, the man described how he had been swimming one summer afternoon with an Indian boy, how the other boy had drowned, and how he had fled the scene, fearful he would be blamed for the death. As time passed, the man said, his fear turned to shame. He could not reemerge looking so foolish. So he went west and lost himself.

Recently, though, he had returned to the area. For nearly a year, he had been living in a Milwaukee hotel, registered as Fritz Lederer, and working on the railroad. To the police and reporters, he spoke of his time away, described the toys he once played with, recalled the vivid details of his "drowning." But his recollections were patchy. He knew what year Fritz's father had died—just two years after the drowning—but could not remember his mother's name. He knew the names of two sisters but did not know how many other siblings Fritz had. He knew that young Fritz played the concertina but struggled to calculate his own age. He said he had wanted to visit his family months before but did not want to go out in the rain. His answers were slow and labored. Few observers thought he was deliberately lying, but even fewer thought he was really Fritz Lederer.

The family was skeptical. The body of Fritz had been recovered in perfect condition only a few hours after the accident. The parents had both identified it as that of their child. But Mrs. Lederer, still weakened with grief after the loss of her son and husband in such succession, wanted to see the man claiming to be her Fritz. A meeting was arranged. Almost immediately after seeing the man, John Lederer recognized him. But not as his long-lost brother. He was a farmhand the family had hired about ten years earlier to cut thistles. The family remembered the man well and for reasons they did not explain had taken to calling him "Crazy Fritz."

The man continued to insist he was the boy in the river that summer afternoon but took their rejection with humor. "Maybe I don't have a name," he told reporters. After the meeting, he was charged with disorderly conduct and held for observation.

MR. BLUNT
July 1893

FRANK BLUNT, twenty-eight years old, was well known among the denizens of the Badlands. Blunt was considered something of a rascal and a rounder, the son of a saloon keeper who was known to have ended at least two marriages with the attention he paid to the wives of other men. His adoptive father, Jessie Blunt, spoke of Frank's wild streak with a kind of pride. "Why, not so very long ago, Frank ran away with a saloon-keeper's wife and they took $450 of the saloon-keeper's money with them," Jessie told a reporter. "The saloon-keeper followed them to Chicago, Oshkosh, and all over, but Frank was too cute for him. Later on, Frank and the saloon-keeper met. They had a footrace around the block, the saloon man following with a revolver."

Perhaps, then, there was little surprise among the Badlanders when Blunt was arrested in July 1893 on larceny charges. Fond du Lac officials were convinced that he had stolen a hundred and fifty dollars from the mother of Jessie Blunt, Frank's adoptive grandmother. When the complaint reached Milwaukee, detectives knew just where to find him, and Blunt quickly found himself at the central station, about to be searched by the station keeper. But just before the officer put his hands on Blunt, the suspect shouted for him to stop. "Don't touch me," he said. "I want the matron to search me." The secret that Frank Blunt had kept for fourteen years was about to be undone. Frank Blunt was a woman.

Frank Blunt was born Annie Morris in Halifax, Nova Scotia. By age thirteen, Annie's home life had grown intolerable. Her mother had died and her father became unbearably cruel. With a younger brother, she ran away to Port Maitland, a little Baptist town about one hundred kilometers north of Halifax. Donning a suit of her brother's clothes, Annie found work in a shoe factory. Sometime during her stay in Port Maitland, her secret was exposed. Jessie Blunt, an itinerant horse trader, just happened to be in town at the time. "When it was discovered that he was a girl, the people became down on him," Jessie said later. "I heard the story and sought out the person and recognized the 'boy' at once. I talked with him and we left the village."

Adopting Annie—now known as Frank—as his own son, Jessie, with Frank in tow, drove a team of horses from Nova Scotia to Boston, and the pair spent the next several years working various jobs up and down the coast. An offer to operate a logging camp took them to northern Wisconsin, where Frank proved himself a rugged and ready man on the job. "I put him to work swamping, driving logs, and teaming. For a time, he also cooked," Jessie said. "Later on, I had to leave on business. Frank was put in charge of the camp and the men. I could not have conducted the business better than he did."

Jessie eventually settled in Milwaukee, running a south-side saloon before buying into the nightlife of the Badlands.

There, Blunt became "one of the boys," a regular at saloons and cafés and a regular seeker of the "company of the women in the district." By his own claim, no one—not even Jessie's family—suspected him to be anything but what he claimed. Blunt's popularity with women, aside from drawing the ire of several husbands, also won him at least three wives of his own. Jessie claimed that his son's first marriage was to a Fond du Lac woman named Lulu Seitz, whom he met shortly after moving to Wisconsin and stayed with for six years—although other sources claimed they stayed together only a month. In March 1892, Blunt's only verified marriage occurred when he was wed to Gertrude Field by a justice of the peace in Eau Claire. Blunt, who was recalled by locals as a "dapper little fellow," ran a restaurant with Field on Eau Claire Street before the couple skipped town, leaving behind a number of unpaid loans. Blunt and Field evidently separated in early 1893. The *Milwaukee Sentinel* reported that three weeks before his arrest, Blunt married Anna Friedburg, the daughter of a wealthy Oshkosh family, whom he brought to Milwaukee and, per the paper, was unaware of his secret.

Blunt's arrest caused a minor sensation, and newspapers from coast to coast reported on the case of the Milwaukee "he-she." As Blunt was arraigned in Fond du Lac and held on five hundred dollars' bail, he still wore his natty cut-away suit and checkered pants. One newspaper wrote of his convincing male stance, noting that "unrestrained by the lace and tight-fitting garments usually worn by her sex, [Blunt's] figure has developed so that [it] is much more masculine than feminine in appearance." It was even reported that he had been a regular voter in Wisconsin since coming of age. "It is safe to say," the *Boston Globe* wrote, "she was the only woman who cast a vote that counted in the last presidential contest."

Unable to make bail, Blunt remained in jail for the duration of the summer, smoking cigarettes and reading novels. So many women tried to visit that the police were forced to amend visitation rules to allow only those guests whom Blunt requested.

One of his most frequent visitors was Gertrude Field, who brought her husband a set of clean shirts and a box of cigars. A newspaper reported that Blunt was grateful, especially for the cigars, and that Field was "a handsome woman [and] just as fond of her he-she husband as ever."

Field was the only of Blunt's wives to emerge after his arrest. Neither she nor her husband made any comment to the press during the affair, but newspapers reported her to be highly "wrought up" over the matter. She even offered to repay from of her own pocket the money Blunt was accused of stealing, but the relationship between Blunt and his extended family was evidently so frayed by his exposure that reconciliation was not possible. After a short trial, funded by Field, Frank Blunt—recognized only as Annie Morris in the official record—was convicted of the crime and sentenced to one year in the penitentiary. Upon hearing the sentence, Field "fell upon the neck of the convict and wept." She vowed to appeal the ruling and take the fight to the state supreme court, but no evidence survives that this was ever done. One year later, Annie Morris left the Fond du Lac jail in feminine dress and was never heard of again.

They Call It Home

SOMEWHERE IN MILWAUKEE a man dressed in cheap pajamas serves drinks behind a long, walnut-top bar. Frank Blunt is there, tipping back whiskeys and making time with the tired gaggle of Bucket of Blood working girls. A group of dandily attired mashers is there, too, tossing affections at a clutch of tittering domestics. They try their act on the overmade and underage girls at the end of the bar as well, but these wide-eyed beauties are not having it. They keep their attention focused on the door, grimacing as they take their drinks and wait for a strapping man in uniform to buy their next round. In the corner of the dusty hall, a sharp in a tailored suit takes numbers for Boss Dalzell and waits for the latest round of winning combinations from Covington. Next to his chair is a locked door. Professor Moebius, violin case in hand and ten bucks burning a hole in his pocket, raps three times on the door and is admitted. In the center of the room, telling bawdy jokes and buying rounds of beer for all his pals, matchstick man Brad Bradley takes mental notes, preparing to swear out a warrant against the place just as soon as he can.

At the police station a few blocks away, as Chief Ellsworth plots a raid of his own, the holding cell is filled to capacity. Barney Farrell tells tall tales of his quixotic conquests to Harry Christiansen and Jiggs Perry. Christiansen's dark glasses conceal the fact that he could not care less while Perry waits impatiently to tell of his own fabricated romances. A pair known only as Daddy and Jack sit together in a corner, each looking guilty as hell but neither saying a word. Herman Hilden sits

calmly on a wooden bench near the overwrought Alice Dornblaser. She is begging him to call out some bingo numbers. In
another corner of the cell, a man tranquilly shaves himself with
a gleaming silver razor while a group of hard-luck Chicagoans
listen with envy to the music, laughter, and sinful groans coming from down the hall. Josephine Willner, specks of blood still
drying on her long, black frock, ignores the goings-on of the cell
as she tiptoes to peek through a barred window. She glares as
Mary Ann Wheeler passes the building in a fine, horse-drawn
carriage. Miss Wheeler is smiling for the first time in months.

Miss Wheeler leaves the jailhouse in her dust and parades
past burning barns, theaters, and hotels. As black smoke
plumes toward the heavens and bodies fall from the sky, Henry
Falk swears he is not entirely to blame. She passes the rail
yards, with doomed and dooming steamers lacing along metal
ribbons. She crosses the river, with tiny bodies floating prone
and ill-fated vessels heading toward an angry lake. The waters churn and thrash, wicked waves grabbing at anything
that crosses them. And yet Captain McKay presses on. As Miss
Wheeler passes through downtown, she sees whorehouses, gambling dens, password saloons, and after-hours clubhouses. On a
River Street corner, Alice Jordan and Susan Fuller trade dirty
looks and foul words. Just blocks south of that tense scene, the
dome of City Hall roars aflame, licking the sky from the highest
point in town. And inside the building's ornate marble halls,
behind brass-knobbed mahogany doors set with heavy etched-
glass windows, Rosina Georg sits in the mayor's office, her feet
up on his desk and her eyes trained out the window, watching
Milwaukee in all its splendid mayhem.

These apparitions are invisible to most. The doomed players
of these stories, and a thousand more that will never be told, go
about their routines as does the city that lives here today. These
stories may be the orphans of history, but they are closer to us
than we think. And no true history of Milwaukee is complete

without them. We cannot fully understand this place without knowing what lives in its underbelly. Even if these men and women were fringe characters of their times, and exist similarly as historical relics today, their tales helped to make this city. As much as did anyone else, these people called it home. And they call it home still.

Notes

Epigraph

Report of the trial of Mary Ann Wheeler, for the murder of John M.W. Lace, her seducer : in the Circuit Court at Milwaukee, Wis., April term, 1853, before Hon. Judge Howe : together with a brief sketch of the life of the prisoner, prepared by a Member of the bar (Sandusky, OH: Bill Cooke and Company's Steam Press, 1853). Yale Law School Legal Scholarship Repository, http://digitalcommons. law.yale.edu/cgi/viewcontent.cgi?article=1010&context=amtrials.

Introduction

H. Russell Austin, *The Milwaukee Story: The Making of an American City* (Milwaukee: The Journal Company, 1946), 14, 39.

MURDER

Slippers at the Cistern

"Mother and Son," *Milwaukee Sentinel*, November 10, 1874.

"Bliss Not Long"

"Suicide of George J. Bunday," *Milwaukee Sentinel*, September 17, 1897; "Bliss Not Long," *Milwaukee Journal*, September 17, 1897; "Maze in Bunday Suicide," *Chicago Tribune*, September 18, 1897; "Will Be Buried Monday," *Chicago Tribune*, September 17, 1897; "Transfers His Property," *Chicago Tribune*, September 18, 1897; "In Mrs. G.A. Bunday's Defense," *Chicago Tribune*, September 23, 1897.

"Our coffins will arrive at your house today..."

"Elopement Ends in Bride's Death," *Chicago Tribune*, January 24,

1905; "Murder," *Milwaukee Journal*, January 25, 1905; "Didn't Have Nerve to Die, He Declares," *Racine Daily Journal*, January 27, 1905; "Of a Calloused Nature," *Racine Daily Journal*, June 2, 1905.

Straight Razor
"Tragical Occurrence in Jail," *Milwaukee Sentinel*, June 3, 1851.

"The Great Judge"
"Death Stops Divorce Trial," *Chicago Tribune*, June 22, 1899; "Aged Husband Shoots Young Wife," *Milwaukee Journal*, June 21, 1899.

The Marrying Brakeman
"Reveal Perry's 'Love Racket,'" *Milwaukee Sentinel*, October 10, 1930; "'T'was a Way with Woman Glib George Perry Had," *Milwaukee Sentinel*, October 10, 1930; "Poverty Faces Perry's Wife," *Milwaukee Sentinel*, October 10, 1930; "Perry Admits Identity," *Milwaukee Sentinel*, May 31, 1931; "'Bride' Spurns Perry," *Milwaukee Sentinel*, June 1, 1931; "Rush Perry Homeward," *Milwaukee Sentinel*, June 2, 1931; "Perry Admits Bigamy," *Milwaukee Sentinel*, June 3, 1931; "Perry Love Racket," *Milwaukee Sentinel*, June 4, 1931; "Fears for Life Keep Wife from Rejoining Perry," *Milwaukee Sentinel*, June 4, 1931; "Perry in Court Today," *Milwaukee Sentinel*, June 5, 1931; "Perry Visited by Wife," *Milwaukee Sentinel*, June 13, 1931; Marv Balousek, "Keys to Her Heart," *50 Wisconsin Crimes of the Century* (Oregon, WI: Badger Books, 1997), 73–76.

Love with a Bullet
"A Boy's Insane Deed," *Milwaukee Journal*, April 5, 1886; "Tragedy in Milwaukee," *Chicago Tribune*, April 6, 1886.

"Don't do that, Harry!"
"Youth Kills Girl and Wounds Self with a Gun at a Drugstore," *Milwaukee Journal*, February 5, 1940; "Rejected Suitor Slays Nurse and Wounds Self in Drugstore Shooting," *Milwaukee Sentinel*, February 6, 1940; "Flash: Girl Shot, Kin's Guess Right," *Milwaukee Sentinel*, February 6, 1940; "Slayer of Girl Fights Death," *Milwaukee Journal*, February 5, 1940; "Slayer of Nurse Is Near Death," *Milwaukee Journal*, February 5, 1940, final edition; "Family of Slayer Is Widely Known in Lumber Trade," *Milwaukee Journal*, February 5, 1940, final edition;

"Blind Youth Gets Life for Slaying Sweetheart," *Chicago Tribune*, July 7, 1940.

A.K.A. Marian Davis
"Poison Verdict Fails to Solve Mystery of Davis Girl's Suicide," *Milwaukee Journal*, February 11, 1921; "Marian Davis Takes Secrets to Her Grave," *Milwaukee Sentinel*, February 11, 1921; "'A Painted Girl' Sends Flowers to Speak for Marian," *Milwaukee Journal*, February 12, 1921; "Kin Claims Poison Girl's Body," *Milwaukee Sentinel*, February 14, 1921; "Perjury in Inquest Charged by Zabel," *Milwaukee Journal*, February 16, 1921; "Marian's Note Tells of Love," *Milwaukee Journal*, February 16, 1921; "Identify Farrell as 'O'Connor,'" *Milwaukee Sentinel*, February 16, 1921; "'Poison Girl' Voices Love for Barney," *Milwaukee Sentinel*, February 16, 1921; "Farrell Changes Story on Stand," *Milwaukee Sentinel*, February 17, 1921; "Farrell Arrested as Result of Inquest," *Milwaukee Journal*, February 18, 1921; "Cleanup of County Is Launched," *Milwaukee Sentinel*, February 21, 1921; "Barney Farrell, Café Prince, Is Now Salesman," *Milwaukee Sentinel*, February 26, 1923.

Leave the Baby
"Confess to Murder," *Chicago Tribune*, July 9, 1893; "The Babe Was Killed," *Milwaukee Journal*, July 8, 1893; "Charged with Murder," *Oshkosh Daily Northwestern*, July 10, 1893; "Mrs. Mill Is Sent Up," *Milwaukee Journal*, March 22, 1894.

Death by Cannon
"Suicide with a Toy," *Milwaukee Journal*, April 9, 1889.

Bingo
"Two Suspects Sought in Woman's Strangling," *Milwaukee Sentinel*, May 7, 1941; "Woman Tenant Confesses That She Killed Teacher," *Milwaukee Sentinel*, May 9, 1941; "Bingo Playing of Defendant Told in Court," *Milwaukee Sentinel*, June 22, 1941; "Death Gloves Are Not Hers, Woman Says," *Milwaukee Journal*, June 24, 1941, final edition; "Takes Blame, but Denies Killing," *Milwaukee Sentinel*, June 25, 1941; "Mrs. Dornblaser Begins Sentence," *Milwaukee Journal*, June 29, 1941.

In a Violinist's Hands
"A Musician's Attempt to Commit Suicide," *Chicago Tribune*, August 25, 1884; *History of Milwaukee, Wisconsin* (Chicago: The Western Historical Company, 1881), 596; "A Would-Be Suicide," *Milwaukee Sentinel*, August 24, 1884.

"Suicide Mania"
"Local Misc.," *Milwaukee Sentinel*, February 5, 1876; "Another Suicide," *Milwaukee Sentinel*, February 11, 1876; "Two Suicides," *Milwaukee Sentinel*, February 12, 1876; "Local Misc.," *Milwaukee Sentinel*, March 4, 1876; "Local Misc.," *Milwaukee Sentinel*, March 20, 1876; "Local Misc.," *Milwaukee Sentinel*, March 21, 1876; "Local Brevities," *Milwaukee Sentinel*, March 22, 1876; "Local Misc.," *Milwaukee Sentinel*, March 22, 1876; "Suicide of a Woman," *Milwaukee Sentinel*, April 24, 1876; "Local Misc.," *Milwaukee Sentinel*, April 28, 1876; "Local Misc.," *Milwaukee Sentinel*, May 8, 1876; "Local Misc.," *Milwaukee Sentinel*, May 11, 1876; "Local Misc.," *Milwaukee Sentinel*, May 19, 1876; "Local Misc.," *Milwaukee Sentinel*, May 29, 1876; "Was It Remorse?" *Milwaukee Sentinel*, May 30, 1876; "The Suicide Mania," *Milwaukee Sentinel*, May 31, 1876; "One More Unfortunate," *The Milwaukee News*, May 31, 1876.

Mrs. Krimmer's Son
"Criminal News," *Chicago Tribune*, September 1, 1881; "Hilden's Crime," *Milwaukee Sentinel*, September 1, 1881; "The Mother's Version," *Milwaukee Sentinel*, September 2, 1881; *The Weekly Wisconsin* (Milwaukee), March 22, 1882; "A Boy Murderer," *Chicago Tribune*, March 15, 1883; "An Interesting Verdict," *Chicago Tribune*, March 24, 1883.

Odors
"Dr. Garner," *Milwaukee Sentinel*, March 3, 1876; "Our Neighbors," *Chicago Tribune*, May 28, 1876; "Dr. John E. Garner," *Milwaukee Free Press*, April 16, 1905, article reprinted at www.linkstothepast. com/milwaukee/mkemarGbios.php#garnerjohne.

"Blood Ends a Feud"
"Blood Ends a Feud," *Milwaukee Sentinel*, April 28, 1895; "Slays Emil Sanger," *Milwaukee Journal*, April 29, 1895; "Challenge to a Duel,"

Milwaukee Journal, July 20, 1895; "He Carried a Dagger," *Milwaukee Journal*, June 13, 1895; Pete Ehrmann, "105 Years Later, Milwaukee Murder Case Still Amazes," *OnMilwaukee.com*, April 21, 2010, www. onmilwaukee.com/buzz/articles/caspersangermurder.html.

"He might have known..."
"Dreadful Tragedy," *Milwaukee Sentinel*, October 15, 1852; "Death of John W. M. Lace," *Milwaukee Sentinel*, October 16, 1852; "The Trial of Mary Ann Wheeler," *Weekly Wisconsin* (Milwaukee), May 25, 1853; Michael Horne, "The Seduction of Mary Ann Wheeler," *Milwaukee Magazine* 13, no. 3 (March 1988): 83–85.

ACCIDENTS

"A Pitiless World"
"A Mystery," *Chicago Tribune*, October 26, 1882; "City News in General," *Milwaukee Sentinel*, October 26, 1882; "Maggie Hennecke," *Logansport (IN) Pharos Tribune*, December 11, 1882; "Wisconsin News," *Oshkosh Daily Northwestern*, December 11, 1882; "Mystery Unraveled," *Newark Daily Advocate*, April 21, 1883; "Milwaukee Mystery Finally Solved," *Freeport Daily Bulletin*, April 21, 1883; "Editorials," *Waukesha Freeman*, April 26, 1883; "Maggie Hennecke," *Milwaukee Sentinel*, April 21, 1883.

Misfire
"The Chapter of Accidents," *Milwaukee Sentinel*, July 6, 1880; "Death of Mamie Van Avery," *Milwaukee Sentinel*, July 7, 1880; "Crowner's 'Quests,'" *Milwaukee Sentinel*, July 8, 1880.

The Fourth
"Careless Celebrants," *Milwaukee Sentinel*, July 5, 1875; "The Fourth," *Milwaukee Sentinel*, July 7, 1875.

"The Ten O'Clock Train"
"Head Cut Off by the Rails," *Milwaukee Sentinel*, July 13, 1893; "Boy Is Beheaded," *Milwaukee Journal*, July 14, 1893.

Switchman

"Seven Killed Instantly," *Milwaukee Journal*, March 2, 1892; "Seven Met Death," *Chicago Tribune*, March 2, 1892; "Coroner's Jury at Work," *Milwaukee Journal*, March 3, 1892; "Emil Barthel Is Quickly Acquitted," *Chicago Tribune*, May 28, 1892.

Collapse

"Railroad Accident," *Milwaukee Sentinel*, March 20, 1876.

Fire in the Sky

R. L. Nailen and James S. Haight, *Beertown Blazes: A Century of Milwaukee Firefighting,* 2nd ed. (Milwaukee: Renaissance Books, 1982), 146–148; "City Hall Tower Wrecked by Fire," *Milwaukee Sentinel*, October 10, 1929; "Crowds Watch Blaze Destroy City Hall Spire," *Milwaukee Journal*, October 10, 1929.

Fire Wild

History of Milwaukee, Wisconsin (Chicago: The Western Historical Company, 1881), 361; "Terrible Conflagration," *Milwaukee Sentinel*, August 25, 1854.

Horror on Main Street

"Terrible Calamity at Milwaukee," *Chicago Tribune*, November 17, 1869; "Terrible Calamity," *Milwaukee Sentinel*, November 16, 1869; "Gaiety Theatre Fire," *Milwaukee Sentinel*, November 17, 1869; *History of Milwaukee, Wisconsin* (Chicago: The Western Historical Company, 1881), 379.

Death's Alley

R. L. Nailen and James S. Haight, *Beertown Blazes: A Century of Milwaukee Firefighting,* 2nd ed. (Milwaukee: Renaissance Books, 1982), 104–106; "Milwaukee Fire Claims 7 Firemen," *Chicago Tribune*, October 27, 1913; "Thousands Groan as Fierce Blast Ends Seven Lives," *Milwaukee Sentinel*, October 27, 1913; "Priest Fights His Way to Dying Men," *Milwaukee Sentinel*, October 27, 1913; "Hospital Is Ready When Dying Arrive," *Milwaukee Sentinel*, October 27, 1913; "Caught in Blast That Rocks City," *Milwaukee Sentinel*, October 27, 1913; "Buried for Hour, Is Rescued Alive," *Milwaukee Sentinel*, October 27,

1913; "Tragic Are Scenes Among Loved Ones," *Milwaukee Sentinel*, October 27, 1913; "Death List Swells to 8," *Milwaukee Sentinel*, October 28, 1913; "Dynamite Blast Killed Firemen," *Milwaukee Sentinel*, November 3, 1913.

Hell Pit at the Davidson

"Nine Brave Men Die," *Chicago Tribune*, April 10, 1894; "Nine Men Killed," *Milwaukee Journal*, April 9, 1894; "The Fall from the Roof," *Milwaukee Journal*, April 9, 1894; "Crowley Is Rescued," *Milwaukee Journal*, April 9, 1894; "Mayor Will Act," *Milwaukee Journal*, April 10, 1894; "The Roof Inquest," *Milwaukee Journal*, April 17, 1894.

The Great Horror

R. L. Nailen and James S. Haight, *Beertown Blazes: A Century of Milwaukee Firefighting*, 2nd ed. (Milwaukee: Renaissance Books, 1982), 78–82; "Horror," *Milwaukee Journal*, January 10, 1883; "Shocking!" *Milwaukee Sentinel*, January 10, 1883; "Vain Hopes," *Milwaukee Sentinel*, January 15, 1883; "Rueful Ruins," *Milwaukee Sentinel*, January 16, 1883; "Arson," *Milwaukee Sentinel*, January 17, 1883; "Secreted," *Milwaukee Sentinel*, January 18, 1883; "Four Additional Bodies," *Milwaukee Sentinel*, January 18, 1883; "The Evidence," *Milwaukee Sentinel*, January 19, 1883; "At the Ruins," *Milwaukee Sentinel*, January 19, 1883; "Care of the Dead," *Milwaukee Sentinel*, January 19, 1883; "The Unidentified Dead," *Milwaukee Sentinel*, January 19, 1883; "The Horror Over," *Milwaukee Sentinel*, January 21, 1883; "Milwaukee's Horror," *Chicago Tribune*, January 17, 1883; "40th Anniversary of the Newhall House Horror," *Milwaukee Journal*, January 7, 1923; "Scheller Acquitted," *Chicago Tribune*, April 18, 1883.

Death on the Queen

"Tank Falls on Excursion Ship," *Milwaukee Journal*, July 1, 1917; "Due to Current, Captain Says," *Milwaukee Journal*, July 1, 1917; "Scenes and Experiences," *Milwaukee Journal*, July 1, 1917; "Boat Disaster Inquest On," *Milwaukee Journal*, August 6, 1917.

The *Alleghany*

History of Milwaukee, Wisconsin (Chicago: The Western Historical Company, 1881), 400; Ruth Kriehn, *The Fisherfolk of Jones Island* (Milwaukee: Milwaukee County Historical Society Press, 1988), 3–4.

"An Ocean Graveyard"
A version of this story appeared in the February 16, 2014, issue of the *Shepherd Express*. "5 Lake Ships Wrecked," *Milwaukee Journal*, October 23, 1929; "Ferry Sunk with 59 Men," *Milwaukee Journal*, October 24, 1929; "Bad Weather Bob Given 50–50 Chance on Safe Trip," *Milwaukee Sentinel*, October 25, 1929; "Carferry Milwaukee Missing, 50 Aboard," *Milwaukee Sentinel*, October 24, 1929; "Waves Smash South Shore Club," *Milwaukee Journal*, October 22, 1929; "Body of Purser of Carferry Identified," *Milwaukee Sentinel*, October 25, 1929.

Launch of the *William H. Wolf*
"Many Were Hurt," *Milwaukee Sentinel*, August 7, 1887; "Launch of the Vessel," *Milwaukee Sentinel*, August 7, 1887; "No More Deaths," *Milwaukee Sentinel*, August 8, 1887; "A Horror in Milwaukee," *Chicago Tribune*, August 7, 1887.

In the Crib
"Death in the Crib," *Milwaukee Journal*, April 20, 1893; "Scenes on the Shore," *Milwaukee Journal*, April 20, 1893; "Found Ten Bodies," *Milwaukee Journal*, April 21, 1893; "An Awful Night," *Milwaukee Journal*, April 21, 1893; "The Crib Disaster," *Milwaukee Journal*, April 21, 1945.

VICE

Games of Chance
"Attack the Police," *Milwaukee Journal*, May 6, 1895; "No Change in Policy," *Milwaukee Journal*, May 6, 1895.

Policy
"Ruining Happy Homes," *Milwaukee Sentinel*, December 11, 1882; "Policy Parasites," *Milwaukee Sentinel*, December 17, 1882; "Dalzell Speaks Plainly," *Milwaukee Sentinel*, March 27, 1883; "Honesty the Best Policy," *Milwaukee Sentinel*, September 15, 1883; "No Policy Played Here," *Milwaukee Sentinel*, September 27, 1885.

Lonely Corners
"Where Vice Runs Riot," *Milwaukee Sentinel*, April 1, 1894; "The Worst Sort of Dives," *Milwaukee Sentinel*, July 18, 1893.

The Queen of Nights
"Additional City Items," *Milwaukee Sentinel*, November 26, 1881; "Minor Notes," *Milwaukee Sentinel*, October 17, 1882; "Rosina Georg Arrested," *Milwaukee Sentinel*, August 24, 1883; "No Local Liquor Law," *Milwaukee Sentinel*, August 25, 1883; "Mallory Criticized," *Milwaukee Sentinel*, August 27, 1883; "A Useful Lawbreaker," *Milwaukee Sentinel*, September 26, 1883; "Rosina Becomes Confidential," *Milwaukee Sentinel*, November 23, 1883; "Editorial," *Milwaukee Sentinel*, November 24, 1883; "Minor Mention," *Milwaukee Sentinel*, February 15, 1884; "Rosina's Place Raided," *Milwaukee Sentinel*, July 14, 1884; "Patrons of Rosina Georg," *Milwaukee Sentinel*, July 15, 1884; "Rosina Georg Convicted," *Milwaukee Sentinel*, July 19, 1884; "Rosina's Bad Record," *Milwaukee Journal*, July 18, 1884; "Rosina's Crew," *Milwaukee Sentinel*, July 20, 1884; "Rosina Twice Guilty," *Milwaukee Journal*, July 24, 1884; "Rosina Georg Twice Fined," *Milwaukee Sentinel*, July 25, 1884; "Rosina in a New Role," *Milwaukee Sentinel*, July 30, 1884; "Municipal Notes," *Milwaukee Sentinel*, August 1, 1884; A Subscriber, letter to the editor, *Milwaukee Sentinel*, August 12, 1884; "Rosina Sells Out," *Milwaukee Sentinel*, August 19, 1884; "Mrs. Georg on Dress Parade," *Milwaukee Sentinel*, September 5, 1884; "Rosina Rammer Stoll," www.findagrave.com, www.findagrave.com/cgi-bin/fg.cgi?page=gr&GRid=116889344.

The Raids
"A Police Raid," *Milwaukee Sentinel*, April 30, 1882.

Protection
"Hush Money," *Milwaukee Sentinel*, August 2, 1884.

With Bells On
"Flappers Use Bells, School Chiefs Balk," *Milwaukee Sentinel*, January 9, 1922; "Shall We Take the Flap out of the Flappers in Milwaukee?" *Milwaukee Journal*, May 6, 1922.

V-Girls and Trouble Boys
"Kerwin Plans Own War on Juvenile Vice," *Milwaukee Sentinel*, July 3, 1943; "Kerwin Plans Vice Cleanup," *Milwaukee Journal*, July 2, 1943; "Many Minors Smoke, Drink," *Milwaukee Journal*, May 11, 1943; "Police Nab Girls in Park," *Milwaukee Journal*, June 18, 1943; "Police Pick Up Seven Girls in Holiday Drive," *Milwaukee Journal*, July 6, 1943; "Venereal Disease in Milwaukee," *Milwaukee Journal*, December 17, 1945; "Jail Is Urged to Curb Vice," *Milwaukee Journal*, October 21, 1943; "Kerwin Plea for Aides to Check Vice Is Argued," *Milwaukee Journal*, July 23, 1943, final edition.

Spoons
"Spooning? Hush!" *Milwaukee Journal Green Sheet*, September 2, 1926; "Canoe Spooning Off; Police Boat Fixed," *Milwaukee Journal*, July 23, 1922; "Milwaukee to Ban Spooning in Canoes," *Pittsburgh Press*, July 24, 1919.

"Kill the Kiss"
"Anti-Kissing Law Is Now Considered," *Milwaukee Sentinel*, June 17, 1912.

Dirty Books
"How He Worked It," *Milwaukee Journal*, December 3, 1891; "A Roast for Comstock," *Milwaukee Journal*, February 1, 1982; "Anthony Comstock Severely Scorned," *Chicago Tribune*, February 2, 1892.

Peppy Tales
"Pair Accused on Filth Sales," *Milwaukee Journal*, April 5, 1941; "Steffes Raids Two Bookstores," *Milwaukee Sentinel*, April 5, 1941; "'Peppy Story' Is Read to Jurors at Trial of Bookstore Man," *Milwaukee Journal*, May 28, 1941, final edition; "Son on Trial on Obscenity Charge," *Milwaukee Sentinel*, May 28, 1941; "Book Sellers Given Terms," *Milwaukee Journal*, May 29, 1941; "Meeting Acts to Stamp Out Unfit Books," *Milwaukee Sentinel*, June 4, 1941.

Orgy at the Workhouse
"Call Four More Witnesses in Probe on Conditions at Workhouse," *Milwaukee Journal*, March 10, 1934; "Open Second Trial of Armin

Kruetzer," *Milwaukee Journal*, May 8, 1933; "May Shut Part of Workhouse," *Milwaukee Journal*, July 18, 1939; "Nude Dance, Dope and Drink at Jail Orgy, Probers Told," *Pittsburgh Press*, March 12, 1934; "Order Momson Suspended," *Milwaukee Sentinel*, March 27, 1934.

"A Speculative Mood"
"In a Speculative Mood," *Milwaukee Sentinel*, July 3, 1872.

Pajamas
"Pajamas Fail to Prevent Dry Raid," *Milwaukee Journal*, December 13, 1932.

Darkness in the Badlands
"Dry Army Swoops Upon City," *Milwaukee Sentinel*, January 7, 1931; "Believe It or Not, the City Is Spotless; All Are Dark," *Milwaukee Sentinel*, January 7, 1931; "38 Liquor Raid Captives Go to Federal Bldg," *Milwaukee Journal*, January 7, 1931.

Black Jack
"Victims of Opium," *Milwaukee Sentinel*, November 21, 1880; "A Nefarious Trade," *Milwaukee Sentinel*, August 21, 1881.

"Now, I don't care."
"Hunt Opium Dens Here," *Milwaukee Sentinel*, September 10, 1934; "Young Woman, Addicted to Narcotics, Looks Like 80," *Milwaukee Journal*, September 10, 1934; "Writs for Five in Opium Case," *Milwaukee Journal*, September 10, 1934; "Find Woman Acted as Dope Informer Six Years Ago," *Milwaukee Sentinel*, September 10, 1934; "Agents Here on Dope Clews," *Milwaukee Sentinel*, September 11, 1934; "Narcotic Drive to Reach City," *Milwaukee Journal*, December 5, 1934; "Gets Stay on Charge of Selling Narcotics," *Milwaukee Journal*, December 7, 1934.

From Chicago
"A Tribute from Chicago," *Milwaukee Sentinel*, May 4, 1866; "Another Contribution from Chicago," *Milwaukee Sentinel*, May 31, 1866; "Police Court," *Milwaukee Sentinel*, July 7, 1866; "Vagrancy," *Milwaukee Sentinel*, July 20, 1866; "Vagrants Sentenced," *Milwaukee Sentinel*, July 26, 1866; "Street Ruffianism," *Milwaukee Sentinel*, July 27,

1866; "A Delectable Trip," *Milwaukee Sentinel*, December 27, 1867; "Police Items," *Milwaukee Sentinel*, August 14, 1868.

The Old Mother's House
"Taking the Law into Their Own Hands," *Milwaukee Sentinel*, August 24, 1858; "Police Court Yesterday," *Milwaukee Sentinel, August* 27, 1858; "An Outrage," *Milwaukee Sentinel*, August 27, 1858; "A Good Riddance," *Milwaukee Sentinel*, August 28, 1858; "Broken Up by the Police," *Milwaukee Sentinel*, August 29, 1860.

River Street Rivals
"Within the Limits," *Milwaukee Sentinel*, August 30, 1875; "The River Streeters," *Milwaukee Sentinel*, September 1, 1875.

Mashers
"Kill the Masher," *Milwaukee Sentinel*, May 18, 1881; "Tramping Trichia," *Milwaukee Sentinel*, May 19, 1881; "A Masher Captured," *Milwaukee Sentinel*, May 25, 1881.

SECRETS

The Vanishers
"Vanishing Rate Here 3 Daily," *Milwaukee Journal Green Sheet*, February 7, 1935.

The Runaways
"Tots Run Away Two Times," *Milwaukee Journal*, September 7, 1898; "Mystery in an Abduction," *Chicago Tribune*, September 7, 1898.

"Am being kidnapped . . ."
"Kidnapping Story of Boy Is Hoax, Police Assert," *Milwaukee Journal*, January 22, 1939; "$20 Snatched, but Not Youth," *Milwaukee Sentinel*, January 22, 1939; "Bank Smiles on Youth's Snatch Hoax," *Wisconsin State Journal* (Madison), January 23, 1939.

The Baby Problem
"Woman Bares Baby Hoax to Help a Friend," *Milwaukee Sentinel*, December 16, 1931.

Woman with a Cut Throat
"Woman's Throat Cut, Leaves Name a Mystery," *Chicago Tribune*, March 30, 1919; "Woman Is Taken off of Train with Throat Slashed," *Milwaukee Evening Sentinel*, March 29, 1919; "Seek Relatives of Woman Found with Her Throat Slashed," *Milwaukee Journal*, March 29, 1919; "Woman Who Slashed Throat Will Recover," *Milwaukee Sentinel*, March 30, 1919.

The Hermit Suicides
"A Sorrowful Suicide," Milwaukee Sentinel, July 12, 1879; "Cases for the Coroner," *Milwaukee Sentinel*, July 14, 1879; "The Hermit Suicides," *Milwaukee Sentinel*, July 21, 1879.

On the Fringe
"City Matters," *Milwaukee Sentinel*, July 31, 1854; "City Matters," *Milwaukee Sentinel*, August 1, 1854; "City Matters," *Milwaukee Sentinel*, August 2, 1854; "Shocking Affair! Shantie Burned," *Wisconsin Patriot*, August 5, 1854.

Bad Man
"Death Warning Mailed to Girl," *Milwaukee Sentinel*, February 26, 1929.

Blind Date
"Seek Two Men in Girl Murder," *Milwaukee Journal*, November 6, 1927; "Lillian Graef, a Fine Girl, Liked to Stay Home," *Milwaukee Journal*, November 6, 1927; "Murder Suspicion Falls on 'Jack,'" *Milwaukee Journal*, November 7, 1927; "Graef Murder Clue Starts Chicago Hunt," *Milwaukee Journal*, November 7, 1927, final edition; "Tip in Girl Slaying," *Milwaukee Sentinel*, November 7, 1927; "Mystery Phone Call Links Rum Fight in Girl Slaying," *Milwaukee Sentinel*, November 8, 1927; "Hi-Jacking Gang Wanted in Second Woman Killing," *Milwaukee Sentinel*, November 9, 1927; "Many Come to Death at Hands of Unknowns," *Milwaukee Sentinel*, November 9, 1927; "Three Grilled in Graef Murder Case," *Milwaukee Sentinel*, November 13, 1927; "Tracing Two Graef Leads," *Milwaukee Journal*, November 20, 1927; "Posters Help Graef Search," *Milwaukee Journal*, December 2, 1927; "Girls Name Graef Suspect," *Milwaukee Sentinel*, January 24, 1928; "7000 to Face Graef Lineup," *Milwaukee Sentinel*, February 17,

1928; "Sister Clears Graef Suspect," *Milwaukee Sentinel*, February 12, 1931.

The Woman at the Breakwater

"Lake Reveals Crime," *Milwaukee Sentinel*, August 4, 1898; "Clue to the Murder," *Milwaukee Sentinel*, August 5, 1898; "Clew to a Dark Crime," *Chicago Tribune*, August 5, 1898; "Seen by a Tug's Crew," *Milwaukee Sentinel*, August 6, 1898; "Police Still Puzzled," *Chicago Tribune*, August 6, 1898; "Small Clues Turn Up," *Milwaukee Sentinel*, August 7, 1898; "Milwaukee Police Hear of Many Missing Women," *Chicago Tribune*, August 7, 1898; "Milwaukee Murder Mystery," *The Daily Journal* (Freeport, IL), August 10, 1898.

Blood Money

"Found Murdered," *Milwaukee Journal*, August 30, 1910; "Young Italian Found with Throat Slashed," *Milwaukee Sentinel*, August 30, 1910; "Killed for $500," *Milwaukee Journal*, August 31, 1910; "Motive for Murder Was Theft of $500," *Milwaukee Sentinel*, August 31, 1910; "Bloody Bill May Be Spoils of Slayer," *Milwaukee Sentinel*, September 1, 1910; Joshua Henze, "Vito Guardalebene and the Early Milwaukee Mafia, 1903–1921," *Informer: The History of American Crime and Law Enforcement* (July 2012): 14–17.

Black Hand

"Dominick [*sic*] Leone Killed by Enemy," *Milwaukee Sentinel*, June 17, 1912; "Italian Leader Slain; Mystery," *Milwaukee Journal*, June 17, 1912; "No Arrests for Murder of Italian," *Milwaukee Sentinel Evening*, June 17, 1912; "Black Hand Work Is Seen in Murder," *Milwaukee Sentinel*, June 18, 1912; "Lips Are Sealed," *Milwaukee Journal*, June 18, 1912; "Attack Is Feared at Leone Funeral," *Milwaukee Sentinel*, June 19, 1912; "I Loved Dominic for His Gentleness," *Milwaukee Journal*, June 19, 1912; "Murder of Leone Causes a Strike," *Milwaukee Sentinel*, July 12, 1912; Joshua Henze, "Vito Guardalebene and the Early Milwaukee Mafia, 1903–1921," *Informer: The History of American Crime and Law Enforcement* (July 2012): 17–20.

The Missing Head

"Discovery of a Headless Skeleton Discloses Old Milwaukee Mystery," *Milwaukee Journal*, January 31, 1953, final edition; "Many Years Dead," *Milwaukee Sentinel*, December 7, 1890.

In the Attic

"Mysterious Affair," *Milwaukee Sentinel*, September 29, 1858.

Not John Dwyer

"Another Body Found in the River," *Milwaukee Sentinel*, April 16, 1855; "Dead Body Found—Probably Murder," *Weekly Wisconsin* (Milwaukee), April 18, 1855; "Body Found on Saturday Not That of John Dwyer," *Milwaukee Sentinel*, April 17, 1855.

"Order of the Day"

"A Mysterious Occurrence," *Milwaukee Sentinel*, July 23, 1856.

The Fortune-Teller

"Local Brevities," *Milwaukee Sentinel*, April 15, 1874; "Local Brevities," *Milwaukee Sentinel*, April 16, 1876; "Local Brevities," *Milwaukee Sentinel*, May 13, 1874; "Local Brevities," *Milwaukee Sentinel*, April 20, 1876; "Local Brevities," *Milwaukee Sentinel*, May 4, 1876; "Local Brevities," *Milwaukee Sentinel*, May 7, 1874; "Local Brevities," *Milwaukee Sentinel*, May 10, 1876.

Heart Failure

"A Milwaukee Romance," *Chicago Tribune*, January 4, 1880.

The Girl Who Couldn't Move

"Milwaukee Girl Who Has Not Spoken or Moved in Five Months," *Chicago Tribune*, December 21, 1898; "Untitled," *Centralia Enterprise and Tribune*, December 24, 1898; "A Girl's Long Trance," *Weekly Wisconsin* (Milwaukee), December 24, 1898; "Hypnotism a Success," *Cedar Rapids Evening Gazette*, December 24, 1898.

The Flying Machine

"Milwaukee's Flying Machine Scare," *Chicago Tribune*, December 7, 1896.

The Old Jarvis House

"Milwaukee's Ghost Mystery," *Chicago Tribune*, June 19, 1898.

The House on the Ravine

"It May Be Rats," *Milwaukee Sentinel*, August 11, 1875.

Incendiary
"Milwaukee Firebug Confesses," *Chicago Tribune*, November 12, 1893.

Crazy Fritz
"Ghost Insists He's Son Buried Two Decades Ago," *Milwaukee Sentinel*, December 18, 1928; "Mystery Man to Face Test," *Milwaukee Journal*, December 19, 1928; "Family Denies Mystery Man," *Milwaukee Journal*, December 20, 1928.

Mr. Blunt
"Frank Blunt a Woman," *Milwaukee Journal*, July 13, 1893; "Frank Blount *[sic]* Is a Woman," *Milwaukee Sentinel*, July 14, 1893; "Annie Morris Voted," *Milwaukee Sentinel*, July 15, 1893; "Fond du Lac," *Milwaukee Sentinel*, July 16, 1893; "Frank Blunt Is Held," *Milwaukee Journal*, July 14, 1893; "Woman in Man's Clothes," *Boston Globe*, July 24, 1893; "Wisconsin News," *Weekly Wisconsin* (Milwaukee), July 29, 1893; "Fond of Marrying," *The Daily Northwestern* (Oshkosh, WI), July 15, 1893; "Fox River Valley Briefs," *The Daily Northwestern* (Oshkosh, WI), July 18, 1893; "Married in Eau Claire," *Eau Claire Free Press Weekly*, July 20, 1893; "Fond du Lac," *The Daily Northwestern* (Oshkosh, WI), August 14, 1893; "Annie Morris Guilty," *Weekly Wisconsin* (Milwaukee), November 25, 1893; "Frank Blunt's Friend Gertie Still Stands by Her," *Eau Claire Free Press Weekly*, January 11, 1894; "Masquerade of Sex," *Milwaukee Journal Sunday Gazette*, February 5, 1933.

Acknowledgments

GROWING UP IN Manitowoc, Wisconsin, I was probably the only ten-year-old boy in the world who dreamed of living in Milwaukee. At that age, my only contact with the city had been the long drives south with my dad to watch the Brewers at old County Stadium. But watching the madness of the place through the car window—the concrete orgies of freeway, the dead-eyed office high-rises, and the charmless tin horseshoe ballpark—I fell into a peculiar kind of love.

It was around that time that Jeffery Dahmer was arrested. The black-and-white details of his horrific decade of carnage delivered to our house every day in the *Milwaukee Sentinel* piqued my interest even further. A car crash was a once-a-year excitement in our neighborhood, but Milwaukee had played host to unspeakable evil for ten years before anyone even noticed. To imagine that people *lived* there, I thought. Big league baseball, lousy traffic, and serial murders.... But I suppose people have been drawn to other places for less.

This is all to say that my appreciation for Milwaukee has never been typical, and that is the driving force behind this book. I wanted to tell the stories that historians had long ignored, but the city—the living, breathing thing that won my heart at an early age—could never really forget. If all the weirdness and horror within these pages makes someone else out there desire for this place, then I'm glad for it. And if it similarly scares someone away, then I'm glad too.

Before I get to the more substantive acknowledgments, I would like to thank a group of people whom I have never met and who had nothing at all to do with this project. Nonetheless, the following people offered much needed distraction and inspiration during the many hours I spent toiling: H. Jon Benjamin, Bette Davis, Bob Dylan, Steve Earle, Erica Gavin, Carlos Gomez, Pam Grier, Drew Magary, Joe Posnanski, Leon Redbone, Crow T. Robot, Chris Rock, James Rolfe, Roseanne, Tom Waits, and Michael K. Williams.

More to the point of this project, I would like to thank the Wisconsin Historical Society Press, particularly Jane De Broux, Sara Phillips, and Kate Thompson, for giving me the chance to tell the kinds of stories I've always wanted to tell. I would also like to thank the staff at the *Shepherd Express*, particularly David Luhrssen, for doing the same. Thanks are similarly due to Jake and Kaila Chianelli and the entire staff and crew at the Milwaukee Boat Line, for their help and support for the Mondo Milwaukee Boat Tour—the adults-only history tour of the city that was the real nexus of this project. Thanks are also due to the University of Wisconsin–Milwaukee history department, particularly professors Joe Austin and Glen Jeansonne, who have taught me that good history need not be dull. Much is owed to Liz Kaune, who edited the early drafts of this work and moved just about every comma I used into its proper place. The resources and staff of the Milwaukee Public Library— especially the staff of the Zeidler Humanities Room—and the Golda Maier Library at UWM were of immense value to this project, as were the many immensely talented journalists who, without bylines, penned the hundreds of resource articles this book used. This book could not have been possible without their florid prose and subtle wit. As in any work, I have stood on the shoulders of giants, specifically Milwaukee historians H. Russell Austin, James Buck, John Gurda, Bayard Still, and Robert Wells.

And of course, I can't forget the many friends and family who have helped me, supported me, or just plain tolerated me during this process. I could not have made it this far without my parents, Ed and Joan, and my little sister, Angie, who always supported even my dumbest ideas. Much love to you all.

And, at the risk of forgetting someone, I'll just say thanks to all those I've hung with, worked beside, whined to, laughed with, laughed at, loved, hated, needed, or forgotten. You know who you are. Make sure to save me a chair at Gee-Wi. Be there just as soon as I get my shoes on.

About the Author

Matthew J. Prigge is a freelance author and historian from Milwaukee and the host of *What Made Milwaukee Famous,* a weekly local history segment on WMSE 91.7. His work has been featured in both local and national publications and has won multiple awards, including the 2013 William Best Hesseltine Award from the Wisconsin Historical Society Press. Since 2011, he has led sightseeing historical tours of Milwaukee's rivers and harbor for the Milwaukee Boat Line. In 2013, he created the Mondo Milwaukee Boat Tour, an evening historical tour of some of the city's most infamous sights. *Milwaukee Mayhem* is his second book.

Index